contents

About Cindi

Cindi Wood is author of LifeWay's bestselling Frazzled Female books. She is sought after as a speaker and Bible teacher, guiding women to deal with daily stress by experiencing a practical and deep relationship with Jesus Christ.

Her Frazzled Female Events have taken her across the United States and into other countries, sharing the good news about Jesus with thousands of busy women who struggle with the many demands of 21st-century living.

Biblically-based teaching coupled with humor from daily experience, her message offers hope and encouragement to women of all ages and walks of life.

Through public appearances, magazine articles, and guest interviews on TV and radio, Cindi's committed passion and lighthearted delivery help women discover joyful living through a deep encounter with Jesus Christ as personal Lord and Savior. Simply reading her titles can bring a smile to your face: *The Frazzled Female* and *Victoriously Frazzled* Bible studies, *Too Blessed For This Mess,* and *I've Used All My Sick Days Now I'll Have To Call In Dead!*

Cindi lives in Kings Mountain, North Carolina, with her husband, Larry. They enjoy ministry partnership with their sons and daughters-in-law. Brandon is a photographer/designer (he's responsible for this book's cover art) living in Nashville, Tennessee *(woodlabelphoto.com* and *indiebling.com).* He and his wife, Bonnie, have one son, Charlie. Lane is on staff at Capital Community Church in Raleigh, North Carolina, as college and student pastor. He has served as a speaker and worship leader across the United States for the past decade *(severelyyours.com).* He and wife, Meg, have two sons, Durham and Ezra.

To find out more about Cindi's ministry or to schedule her to speak in your area, contact Regal Ventures at (800) 282-2561. You may also visit Cindi Wood on Facebook at *www.cindiwoodfacebook.info* and at *www.frazzledfemale.com*

Desperate

LifeWay Press®
Nashville, Tennessee

Published by LifeWay Press® • © 2012 Cindi Wood

ISBN 978-1-4158-6999-4 • Item 005376431

Dewey decimal classification: 248.84 • Subject headings: SPIRITUAL LIFE \ JESUS CHRIST--PASSION \ WOMEN

Cover design by Brandon Wood *(woodlabelphoto.com and indiebling.com)*

To order, write to LifeWay Church Resources Customer Service; One LifeWay Plaza; Nashville, TN 37234-0013; fax (615) 251-5933; phone (800) 458-2772; e-mail *orderentry@lifeway.com;* order online at *www.lifeway.com;* or visit the LifeWay Christian Store serving you.

Printed in the United States of America

Leadership and Adult Publishing
LifeWay Church Resources
One LifeWay Plaza
Nashville, TN 37234-0175

Introduction

Are you desperate to make your life more manageable? Discover the power of the cross. Jesus said: "Whoever wants to save [her] life will lose it, but whoever loses [her] life because of Me will find it" (Matt. 16:25). My life has been transformed as I've researched Scripture, prepared content, and worshiped our Lord in preparation for this study. In my quest for simplicity, I've discovered the cross. Its truth has changed the way I approach life. Stress remains, but Jesus is greater.

As you journey through *Desperate,* don't let it be merely another item on your to-do list. Rather, expect God's Word to enlighten and refresh you. Its content is rich and life-changing if you meditate and savor its message. Allow the hymns to be part of your worship. God's Spirit may lead you to spend a week with one day or to take weeks for one section. Seek God's heart in new and fresh ways. Perhaps in the past you've joined the ranks of Bible-study dropouts. The pressure's off. You can be a diligent student without being fast-paced or stressed-out. Whether one-on-one with the Lord or taking a sister approach, design a format suitable to you.

Instead of including a weekly memory verse, you'll find "The Scripture Garden" on pages 134–35. Reflect and meditate on passages that go along with the weekly content. God's Word is full of verses to enjoy and memorize. The Scripture Garden will provide a starting place, or you may explore His Word on your own. Whatever your approach, it's critical and life-changing to memorize God's Word.

I pray this study will draw you deeper into relationship with God. It's especially when you're desperately holding on to your sanity by a thread that God wants you to turn His way and hear Him speak. Imagine this conversation:

> *"Lord, my mind is in a whirlpool of daily pressures and stress."* — **"I can handle that."**
> *"My emotions seem untethered to Your stability."* — **"I'll help you."**
> *"My schedule is slam-packed."* — **"I understand."**
> *"I'm often distracted, disturbed, and sometimes depressed."* — **"I know where you live."**
> *"I long for Your peace and joy. I need a real purpose for living."* — **"Do you love Me?"**
> *"Oh yes, Lord. I do love You!"* — **"Take My hand; let's go."**

Dear Friend, if you've never begun a relationship with Him, your salvation is a done deal, waiting for you to accept. Joy, peace, and purposeful living await you in a relationship with Christ. Turn to page 133 to begin the journey of a lifetime. You can choose to redefine your life. The journey begins at the cross!

Enjoying His Grace,

Jesus Loves Me

Jesus loves me! this I know,

For the Bible tells me so;

Little ones to Him belong;

They are weak, but He is strong.*

Lord, You love me when I'm stressed,

even tho' my life's a mess.

When I give it all to You,

You will always see me through.**

Yes, Jesus loves me,

Yes, Jesus loves me,

Yes, Jesus loves me,

The Bible tells me so.*

—Anna B. Warner, 1860*

**author's words

1

my life's
driving me
crazy!

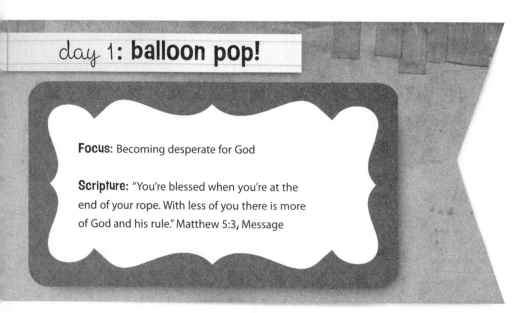

day 1: **balloon pop!**

Focus: Becoming desperate for God

Scripture: "You're blessed when you're at the end of your rope. With less of you there is more of God and his rule." Matthew 5:3, Message

embarrassed

For real, I am. Even so, I need to be straight up with you. I want you to know I have experiential knowledge of what's at stake when stress turns you into a victim, arms flailing and words spewing, while those on the sidelines shriek back in horror or worse yet, laugh. Actually, I have many such memories, but one particular day springs to mind when I think over those many times I lost it.

First, imagine you are a latex balloon (a red-hot one of course). Each stress event in your day deposits a puff of air into you—the balloon. Here's my real-life scenario and how it all went down.

My then 13-year-old son Brandon and I were finally on the homeward trek after a difficult day at the middle school where I taught and where he was in seventh grade. Lots of opportunities throughout my teaching day puffed those stressors into my balloon. Students bickering, parents calling, interrupted schedules, and unexpected reports had greatly increased my stress load since we'd left home at 6:30 a.m.

We were running on a tight schedule and had just enough time to get home, grab a bite to eat, and head out the door for the Little Theater production starring my son as lead character. Proud mama? Yes, but agitation was trumping the pride. There was no time for a hiccup in our plans. Tension mounting, nerves fraying … let the countdown begin.

Brandon took a note out of his book bag. 5! "Mom, I need a pair of white socks for the play tonight." 4! "What? Why am I just now hearing this?" 3! "I didn't mention it because I thought I had white socks!" 2! "You do have white socks!" 1! "Mama, I thought I did, but I don't have any white socks!" 0!

Balloon pop. It's over!

Calm mom. Usually even-tempered mom explodes when the white-sock agitator pushes her over the edge. I don't need to describe the explosion. You know what it looks like, sounds like, and how unforgettable it is for all who experience it. So, what are typical agitators for today's busy woman?

Anything, everything.

As fate would have it, the one that pops your balloon is often something insignificant. You see, it's not the thing itself. It's the fact that this one just happened to be at the end of a long string of stress harassers; and you, the balloon, have been stretched to your limit and can't deal with one more little bitty thing.

Has your balloon ever popped? ☑ yes ○ no

If yes, underline the words or phrases that describe how you felt afterward.

<u>embarrassed</u>	sad	silly	<u>ashamed</u>	helpless
angry	worthless	<u>out of control</u>	low-down	other _____

they pile up

Stressors, I'm talking about. You know ... those little irritants that poke at your soul like little pin sticks. A couple or so don't bother you; you barely notice. Actually, you've gotten pretty good at making it through your day, paying little attention to all those trivial annoyances that add up until somebody gets on your last nerve, the headache that's been germinating all day finally sprouts, or the last e-mail of the workday sends you over the edge and suddenly you just can't take it anymore.

Circle the stressors or list others that have poked at your nerves.

uncooperative family	computer blips	clothes too tight
running late for work	crowded food store	bad hair day
others whining	waiting in long lines	interrupted sleep
too many phone calls	no time for self	a Facebook comment
other _____		

Most women I know truly do not want their balloon to pop. Busy women. Busy, good women long to exude happiness and self-control. They want their children, grandchildren, husbands, friends, and the people they brush by during the day to sense someone who is a confident manager of life's stresses.

But mostly, they want to experience it themselves. Ohhh, the longing to really experience daily peace and fulfillment—and in the middle of a hectic lifestyle. During the 21st century, do we dare dream that it's possible to live a life free from the bondage of stress?

Check each statement that applies to you.
- ○ **Most days I live in stress-overload.**
- ○ **It's rare to feel that life is stressful.**
- ○ **Little things annoy me in big ways.**
- ○ **Daily stress is my new normal.**
- ○ **I desperately want my life to be peaceful and fulfilling.**

the first step

From one who is a daily seeker of peace, joy, and fulfillment, I can tell you the first critical step is a desperation for your heart to mesh with the heart of God. For much of my life, stress has had a hold on me. I've tried to prevent it, manage it, organize it, and pray it away. Not until I became desperate to know God, instead of being desperate to get rid of stress, did life really begin to change.

I don't understand it, but I know it's true. For me, God used the overload of stress in my life to reveal His Glory. What a blessing. I'm living proof that coming to the end of your rope can be a blessed event but only when it drives you to God's heart.

Right now, is your heart aching for a saner lifestyle? What are you feeling?

My friend, get excited. You're in the midst of a God encounter. That stirring is His Holy Spirit gently pulling you toward the realization that life can be better than it is and sweeter than you can imagine. He's longing to fill you with hope and new direction right in the middle of your balloon pop. That's the kind of God He is.

Think about how God might use your stress to bring you closer to His heart. Can you sense His love for you as you struggle to do good things? Are you confused about what and how you can let go of some of these things?

Worship with this week's hymn, and scribble your thoughts.

Dear Father, I finally admit it. I'm desperate for You to bring peace into my life. I know my efforts can't do it, and my love alone is not enough. I honestly don't understand how to deal with all of the stress that's in my life, so I come to You helpless and needy. You have promised to bless me when I turn to You. Here I am. I love You.

day 2: here comes Jesus!

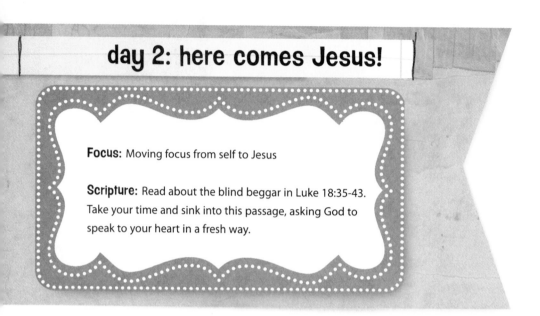

Focus: Moving focus from self to Jesus

Scripture: Read about the blind beggar in Luke 18:35-43. Take your time and sink into this passage, asking God to speak to your heart in a fresh way.

Some commentaries refer to the blind beggar as Bartimaeus, but Luke simply calls him "a blind man." His identity and name may be uncertain, but he's a favorite biblical hero to me. What does he do that ranks him at the top? He simply cries out to Jesus. Unstoppable and relentless crying out to the Messiah, until He looks his way.

Blind, poor, and a beggar; he's done with it all. His loud and insistent cry for help won't be squelched. He's neither intimidated nor willing to bow down to the crowd who tells him to shut up. No. This man's had it. He's crying out to the only One who can save him. His cry of desperation gets my attention, but more importantly, it gets the attention of Jesus.

Are you at that "can't-take-it-anymore" place? Check the statements that most accurately describe how you feel now or how you've felt in the past.
- ○ I can't deal with one more thing.
- ○ I keep trying to _____, but it's futile.
- ○ Nothing seems to be working.
- ○ I feel like I'm going crazy.
- ○ If only I had a little help.
- ○ God seems silent.

worse than terrible

Beggars were often seen at the city gate where people went in and out. This poor blind man was probably used to calling out to those who passed by, asking for money and begging for alms. And he'd probably done so for much of his life.

The image of this man begging for help and attention tugs at my heart. A real person, loved by God, but often overlooked and dismissed by others. Can you imagine his low self-esteem heaped on top of being so physically needy? Being a pauper and totally dependent upon the wealth and goodness of passersby, he surely felt destitute of love of self and others.

Feeling like you're at the end of your rope can lead to self-absorption—which leads to physical and emotional manifestations.

Underline any you've experienced.

loss of sleep	physical pains	emotional depletion
loss of joy	uneasiness	extreme fatigue
restlessness	lack of desire	lack of concentration
anger	instability	other _____

Day in and day out, he dragged his tired body and positioned it where he could best be seen and heard. Not able to work because he was blind, he sat by the wayside begging. Blind, poor, and miserable, he sat … and sat … and sat … until one day, here came Jesus! From the noise and chaos, he could tell the crowd was much larger than usual. The pushing and shoving prompted him to cry out to whoever could hear him, "What's going on?"

Then one in the crowd shouted back, "Jesus of Nazareth is passing by!"

Can you imagine the trickle of hope that began to percolate deep inside his heart? A small anticipation that there could possibly be a proverbial light at the end of his long dark tunnel?

How does the hope of Jesus healing you physically, emotionally, or mentally make you feel? Circle all that apply.

excited	relieved	energized	grateful	undeserving
valuable	hopeful	honored	loved	comforted
eager for a fresh start		lighthearted		

Do you believe Jesus knows all of your needs and longs for you to experience these things? ○ yes ○ no

Explain your response.

faith crying

Realizing it was Jesus passing by, our blind friend began yelling at the top of his lungs, "Jesus, Son of David, have mercy on me!" (v. 38). Those surrounding him rebuked him and tried to stifle his cries, but he shouted all the louder, "Son of David, have mercy on me!" (v. 39).

The Greek translation of "have mercy" in this passage means to "have compassion."[1] The reputation of Jesus had surely preceded Him. This man's plea was no helpless, feeble cry. It was loud and insistent. He surely hoped to get the attention of One who might possibly look on him with compassion instead of disgust. As he cried out to Jesus, the opinions of others simply did not matter.

Have you ever been caught up in what others may think of you when you're going through difficult times? What have you assumed they were thinking?
- ○ She doesn't have enough faith.
- ○ She thinks things are worse than they are.
- ○ She could do something to make things better.
- ○ She brought it on herself.
- ○ She deserves what she's getting.
- ○ She can't handle tough situations.
- ○ She attracts trouble.

My friend, there's One who understands you and everything you're experiencing right now. On top of that, He loves you through and through and wants you to know it.

The blind beggar was just that; blind and begging. At the moment Jesus passed by, he readjusted his focus, from physical blindness to being blind to everyone and everything except Jesus. He went from begging for handouts to begging for healing. He set his mind and attention on the only One who could really help him.

You can do the very same thing, right now. At this moment, you can block out everyone and everything and simply set your mind and attention on the only One who can really help you, Jesus.

As you close today's study, position yourself as the blind beggar. Reach out to Jesus and see Him tenderly turn your way as He hears your cry for help.

Worship with this week's hymn, and scribble your thoughts.

Dear Lord, oh how I need You. Right now I'm choosing to let go of my self-effort. Right now I'm choosing to let go of being consumed with what others think. I'm simply crying out to You to save me. Please help me to readjust my focus to You and Your love for me. I love You.

day 3: daily "to-do" things

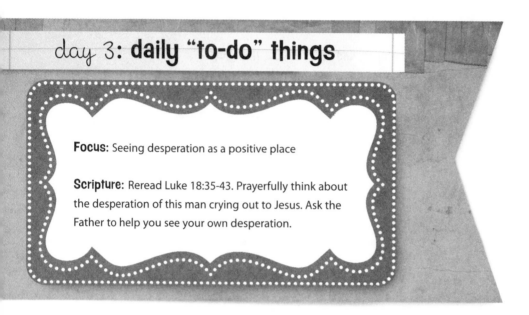

Focus: Seeing desperation as a positive place

Scripture: Reread Luke 18:35-43. Prayerfully think about the desperation of this man crying out to Jesus. Ask the Father to help you see your own desperation.

My times of desperation seem to fall in one of two categories: accumulation of daily stuff and major life events.

Accumulation of daily stuff involves "today things" spilling over to the next day, then the next, and the next … until I feel paralyzed and unable to move forward toward completion.

Major life events are happy, exciting times or heartbreaking occasions that open the door to extreme emotions. Marriage, births of children and grandchildren, buying a new home, death of loved ones, and career change are some of the major life events I've experienced.

We'll explore these categories today and tomorrow. I want to help you realize that whether you slide into desperation gradually or are catapulted from the spring-board of stress, this can be a great place if it brings you to the end of self.

Remember—"You're blessed when you're at the end of your rope. With less of you there is more of God and his rule" (Matt. 5:3, Message).

daily things

I'm a planner—big time. Having things all planned out gives me a sense of control and organization. Proper planning of my daily schedule helps me be more efficient in managing my time and energy. Now this works out just great as long as I'm in control of my plans. What doesn't work is when my planning depends on the planning of others and their plans don't go along with mine. Get the picture?

Have your plans ever been contingent on the plans of others? ⊘ yes ○ no
If yes, what was the situation?

Going to bible study over letting Amanda help clean my house for her party. I could be helpful to her by not going but then if interfers w/ my comm. to this bible study

Explain how you felt not being in control of your plans.

I hate feeling guilty about choosing this over that but I'm trying to make this a priority in my life.

Awaiting the birth of my first grandson gave me practice in the "others are not cooperating with my plans" department. We were about a month out. Baby's mom was 35 weeks and holding, and I was about to go into labor. I was entering into a new phase of life and there was nothing easy about it. My birthing pangs were coming fast and furious.

Oh yes, I was desperate! Desperate because I was going nuts trying to get on top of all the daily things that had to be done before I became a grandmama. It was not the birth of our baby that had me stressed out but the many things I had to attend to before he arrived, during his arrival, and in the months after he arrived. Many unknowns revolved around the completion of my list.

Place an X in the area that best describes how often you get stressed out over your to-do list.

never	weekly	monthly	pretty much all the time

Has your daily to-do list ever driven you to panic mode? ⊘ yes ○ no

Circle words and phrases describing how you felt.

anxious	afraid	hopeless	agitated	helpless
worn out	uncertain	angry	useless	attacked
done with it all	wishing for help			

Desperation can be your turning point. Refresh your mental image of the blind beggar screaming for Jesus. His was an irrepressible desire that kept him shouting louder and louder, "Jesus, Son of David, have mercy on me!" (Luke 18:38).

He knew what he wanted, and he was going after it. His cry was not directed to just anyone, but to the One who could restore his sight. "Son of David" as a title is equivalent to "Messiah," as it signifies to the Jews a person who is the promised descendent of David who will sit upon Israel's throne.[2]

He'd cried out countless times to others, hoping for physical relief from his poverty and hunger. On any given day, that was the best he could hope for. But now Jesus was passing by. By reputation, he knew this One was capable of giving much more than temporary relief. His was the gift of total healing.

Do you see the progression? Because of hard times (blind, hungry, and poor) he was positioned (physically and emotionally) to become utterly desperate for Jesus to meet his needs. If he hadn't been desperate he may have totally missed it. Desperation becomes a great place when it causes you to cry out to Jesus, the only One who can save you.

Has the accumulation of daily stress ever caused you to be desperate for Jesus?
⊘ yes ○ no

Explain your answer below.

> Tuff ran away right before bed causing me to be desperate and I fell to the floor and cried to him. The stresses of the day had piled up.

When you become desperate for Jesus in day-to-day activities, you will focus more on His love and grace than you do when you move in your strength and ability. By calling out to Him and recognizing Him as your Savior from daily stress, you'll begin to experience more peace and joy as you work through the issues before you.

Circle the day-to-day areas where you'd like to experience more joy and peace.

paying bills	getting groceries	working
exercising	cooking meals	caring for parents
going to church	devotional time	cleaning the house
caring for children	running errands	family time

Fortunately, before my grandbaby was born, I finally came to the end of self-effort. I laid my agenda aside, trusting my Heavenly Father to guide me and pull everything together for me.

Before this desperation led me to Jesus, I felt distracted, discouraged, and depleted. When I finally admitted there was no way I could get all of these unknowns resolved on paper, I gave my list totally to Him. The unknowns were still there, but I moved from panic to peace. I can't fully explain it, but I sure did gratefully receive it. I spread my arms open and upward, giving Him full access to my heart, my mind, and my plans.

My desperation led me to Jesus. I gradually began to feel focused, encouraged, and energized.

Dear friend, a life full of too much to do and too many to take care of can hurl you into despair. That's a horrible and hopeless place to live. The great news is that you don't have to stay there. Just take the next step into God's provision. Relinquish your need to control it all, and let Him work it out. When you do this, you step into His peace. His peace will carry you through the days ahead. His peace will help you think more clearly, placing the burden of it all on Him, not you.

Want Him to take over?

Worship with this week's hymn, and scribble your thoughts.

Dear Father, I'm gradually understanding how being desperate can be a good thing. Thank You for revealing Your love to me. Thank You for helping me understand that when I'm at the end of my rope, I'm brushing against Your heart. I love You.

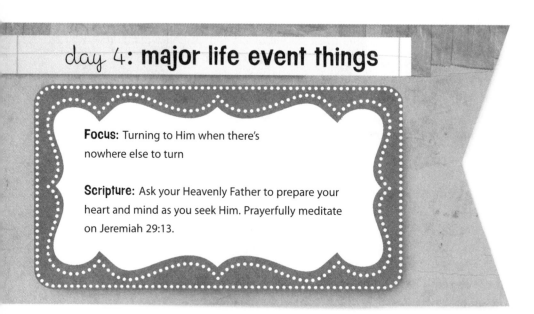

day 4: **major life event things**

Focus: Turning to Him when there's nowhere else to turn

Scripture: Ask your Heavenly Father to prepare your heart and mind as you seek Him. Prayerfully meditate on Jeremiah 29:13.

a healing miracle

Years ago, my mom and I shared an incredible experience. This particular morning, I sat by her side where she was an oncology patient at Presbyterian Hospital in Charlotte, North Carolina. When she left for tests, I found my way to the hospital's chapel. As my prayers gave way to tears, I didn't pay attention to the entrance of the man who rocked our world. Phasing out of my meltdown, I noticed him: quietly poised with clergy attire flowing under a kind, gentle face.

It was one of those days when I needed to talk. So when he asked, "What's troubling you?" I poured forth with volcanic gusto. It felt so good to have someone to share this burden.

Place a check by feelings you've experienced after pouring your heart out.

- ○ relief
- ○ joy
- ○ freedom
- ○ renewal
- ○ embarrassment
- ○ strength
- ○ affirmation
- ○ other _____
- ○ depletion
- ○ encouragement
- ○ understanding

My clergy friend then introduced himself as Leroy and invited me to continue. After I described the mass of cancer and the next phase of testing, Leroy simply said, "Tomorrow the tests will reveal that the cancer is not there."

That was it. No explanation, no wavering, just a statement of fact.

The next day, it happened just as he'd said. My mom and I were stunned—joyful, but stunned. We immediately set out to find Leroy, the hospital chaplain. Staff directory—no record of his name. Volunteer register—not there. Ministry logbook where dates and times are logged with names of ministers—no listing of Leroy and no one recognizing him by the description I gave. After exhausting our search efforts, my mom and I hugged and thanked our Heavenly Father for this angel of ministry who had foretold her healing.

Have you had an unexplainable encounter? If so, briefly describe your experience.

The next months provided many opportunities to share this miracle story. Mom and I together told the story of Leroy and the cancer disappearing just as he said it would. God was glorified in the telling and the rejoicing that followed each sharing.

the unexpected

Three months after the miracle of "no cancer" occurred, the cancer returned. Without announcement or warning, it was back. As blown away as we were by its disappearance, the recurrence of this deadly disease left us even more dumbstruck.

Why would God do such a thing? Why would He allow or even orchestrate such an event so miraculous, only to seemingly unravel the reports of glorious healing? From the depths of my heart I wondered and cried.

Why did God take back our miracle? It would have been far better if we'd never experienced this miracle of healing. I couldn't find a Bible verse to help me deal with this pain. The hurt I felt almost made me feel betrayed.

Have you ever felt betrayed by God? ○ yes ○ no

If yes, place a check by the area in which you experienced these feelings.
○ end of marriage   ○ difficulty with children   ○ infertility
○ miscarriage   ○ death of a loved one   ○ rejection
○ loss of job   ○ health issues   ○ other _____

What were the cries from the depths of your heart?
1.

2.

3.

desperate

As my heart cried out to my God, one thought surfaced again and again—fear!

Not fear of cancer or of the journey ahead. Not even fearful of losing my mom to earthly death. The one consuming thought that strangled my peace and sent me into panic mode was this: *I was afraid of losing my intimacy with God.*

In all my earnest attempts to make sense of this latest development and to understand why God would allow such a tragedy, I simply could not. My heart was void of consolation and resolution. The sweetness I'd experienced with my Savior seemed vague and far away. I wanted Him to make it all OK but couldn't sense how He possibly could.

Second Corinthians 4:8-10 comes to mind now, as I still recall the pain of that ordeal. "We are pressured in every way but not crushed; we are perplexed but not in despair; we are persecuted but not abandoned; we are struck down but not destroyed. We always carry the death of Jesus in our body, so that the life of Jesus may also be revealed in our body."

I *felt* crushed and abandoned, but I knew I was not. In the numbness of the moment the only thing I seemed able to do was to grab hold of Jesus. The stench of death surrounded me, and I was desperate for Jesus to renew me with His thinking, His direction, His life.

And so I cried to Jesus. In planting my emotional and physical feet, I placed every ounce of energy I had in crying out to the only One who could bring resolution to my anguished soul. It was an intense time, an urgent and deliberate time of pouring my heart out steadfastly to Him. It seemed God had placed me in such a position of having nowhere to turn except to Him.

Has God ever placed you where you had nowhere to turn except to Him?
○ **yes** ○ **no**

If yes, explain.

from desperation to peace

For three long and desperate weeks, I cried out to Him, steadfastly planting my heart and soul before Him. I stopped asking questions and trying to make sense of it all. I simply cried out His name.

Jesus!

Then, after weeks of desperately crying out, I simply stepped into His peace. I can't explain it. To this day I cannot describe the spiritual nuts and bolts of how it happened. I only know it did. And when His peace was ushered in, it came completely and undividedly. One moment, utterly desperate. The next, totally peaced-out.

Mom's heavenly entrance marked her earthly time line shortly after this event. Oh, the peace that certainly engulfed her. Jesus, her peace, her comfort, her answer.

For me, I discovered that in the midst of my cries for explanation, He gave me Himself and He was all I needed. Jesus, my peace, my comfort, my answer.

My friend, tenaciously crying out to Jesus with a sincere and genuine heart will usher you into His peace. He is the source of peace whether your circumstance is resolved here on earth or later in heaven. He alone is your peace. His life stirs within you, filling you with hope and unexplainable joy—His joy. Are you desperate for His touch today? Do you need Him to be your answer for a troubling and uncertain time of life?

Worship with this week's hymn, and scribble your thoughts.

Dear Father, I need You to make it all OK. Give me strength to stand firm and call out Your name. Help me know You are my answer. I love You.

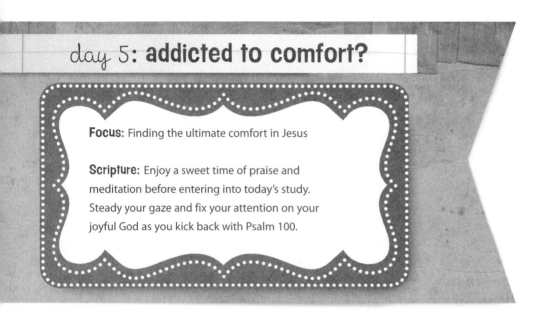

day 5: **addicted to comfort?**

Focus: Finding the ultimate comfort in Jesus

Scripture: Enjoy a sweet time of praise and meditation before entering into today's study. Steady your gaze and fix your attention on your joyful God as you kick back with Psalm 100.

chocolate, shoes, or Jesus?

Have you ever noticed God's sense of humor? I sure did the moment He revealed to me my addiction to comfort, or to be exact, coffee.

It happened when I was putting the final touches on a message about desiring Jesus. Early that morning, I'd headed down to the hotel lobby to grab a cup of freshly brewed, just right for me, cup o' java. When I reached the coffee bar, the words "Our coffee pot is broken" gave me fresh energy to sprint back up the stairs to my hotel room and plug in the little one tucked inside the closet. After two failed attempts of trying to resuscitate the long dead pint-sized version of a pot, He spoke.

"Are you as desperate for *Me* as you are for that cup of coffee?"

There it was. Loud and clear from the heart of the Lover of my soul. He'd shut me down with broken coffee pots to reveal my desire for lesser things.

Now you may be thinking this is no big deal. *It's just a cup of coffee.* But stay with me. If you're truly interested in going deeper with Him, you'll give some serious thought to this concept. Truth is, you could be missing out on some mega-charged blessings by turning to other people and other things to get your wants met. God designed it that way, you know. He's a jealous God and wants to be the first on your list of where to turn when life leaves you lacking. That yearning in your heart that will not be satisfied is from Him.

It's not only about needs, it's about wants. You were created with a hungering in your spirit not only to need God but also to want Him—to want Him more than you want anybody or anything. He put that craving there; it's from Him.

"The LORD your God is a consuming fire, a jealous God!" (Deut. 4:24).

On this final day of week one, we are looking at comfort addictions. Is every "want for comfort" you experience ultimately fulfilled in your love relationship with Jesus or in other things or other people? My goal is not to douse you with guilt, nor mute your enjoyment of life's pleasures. Oh no! I simply want to give you some food for thought so that you'll notice your subtle desires for lesser things. What do you get a hankering for when you'd like a little pick-me-up? What craving pops into your mind when you want some umpff to your day? In other words:

What scratches your itch? Check your answers and explain.
○ **Food. What kind?**
○ **Shopping. For what and where?**
○ **Getting away. Where?**
○ **Entertainment. What sort?**
○ **Other** _____

got satisfaction?

Sometimes no matter what we do, no matter what we try, no matter how hard we work, or no matter what things we have, we just don't feel satisfied with our lives.

Where's your satisfaction deficiency? Briefly describe below. Skip any that don't apply. (For example, Family: I wish my husband just enjoyed talking with me.)
Family:

Church:

Career:

Friendships:

Other:

Here's the biblical truth: God "has planted eternity in the human heart" (Eccl. 3:11, NLT). Deep inside us is a craving that cannot and will not be satisfied with any earthly thing.

In thinking about getting our desires met, I'm not addressing the many sinful places we might turn. I'm talking about the relatively harmless ones, those superficial, instant-gratification places.

Every time we reach for that special something to appease our insatiable whim of the moment, we recognize there's a little something lacking in the satisfaction department. Craving and grabbing a piece of chocolate feels gratifying for the moment but soon leaves us pining again. We simply have this deep-seated drive to get our wants and needs met. There's a hunger that will not be totally satisfied and a thirst that will not be totally quenched. Even as believers, our hearts still long for something richer and deeper and grander.

Perhaps you're thinking it's a bit far fetched to link such insignificant desires with your passion for God. After all, they are a bit benign in and of themselves. That's true, but let me encourage you to delve a bit deeper. During the weeks following my coffee episode, I began noticing subtle cravings that I had not paid attention to before. Some had to do with food; some with other "fixes" like shopping or driving somewhere. I began talking to God during these impulses saying something like, "Lord, right now I'm turning to You with this appetite, instead of to _____."

Each time I forfeited the lesser desire for the Higher One, I sensed pleasure in my Father's heart. It wasn't that He was demanding this gift, but He seemed pleased that during this particular moment I preferred Him over His gifts to me.

Answer the following statements with *yes*, *no*, or *s* (for sometimes).
_____ **I enjoy God's gifts to me more than I enjoy the relationship we share.**
_____ **His gifts satisfy me more than His presence.**
_____ **God's most precious gifts to me substitute for deeper intimacy with Him.**
_____ **I am aware of reaching for other pleasures instead of for God's company.**
_____ **I lack deep satisfaction in my life.**
_____ **A deeper hunger for God is growing in my heart.**

the big cover-up

I encourage you, dear sister, to take a look inside yourself. Could you possibly be covering up unhappiness, guilt, fear, boredom, or anger with food and other things? Are you looking to these things for temporary satisfaction instead of finding ultimate satisfaction inside God's heart? I hope today's study will help you ponder a bit and bring refreshment to your spiritual journey. By all means, savor that piece of chocolate and cup of coffee. But instead of turning to them for comfort, let them be an opportunity to praise the Giver. "Delight yourself in the LORD and he will give you the desires of your heart" (Ps. 37:4, NIV).

As we close this week's study, consider the essence of today's subject. Decide if you want to take this challenge to press in a bit and explore this notion of channeling your whimsical desires toward God's heart instead of toward lesser sources of happiness and comfort.

Worship with this week's hymn, and scribble your thoughts.

Dear Heavenly Father, I want to go deeper with You. Please, Holy Spirit, reveal Your truth. Am I enjoying Your gifts more than I'm enjoying You? Draw me to Your heart. Show me how to love You more. I'm listening with excitement. I love You.

1. "Mercy," *Word Study Tool* [online, cited 23 January 2012]. Available from the Internet: *www.mystudybible.com*
2. *HCSB Study Bible* (Nashville, TN: Holman Bible Publishers, 2010), 1776.

At Calvary

Years I spent in vanity and pride,

Caring not my Lord was crucified,

Knowing not it was for me He died

On Calvary.

Now I've given to Jesus everything,

Now I gladly own Him as my King;

Now my raptured soul can only sing

Of Calvary.

Mercy there was great, and grace was free;

Pardon there was multiplied to me;

There my burdened soul found liberty,

At Calvary.

—William R. Newel, 1895

2

cross examination

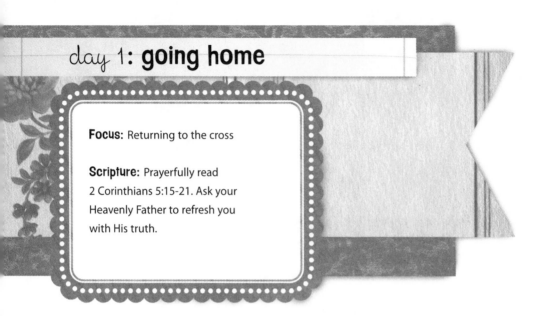

day 1: **going home**

Focus: Returning to the cross

Scripture: Prayerfully read
2 Corinthians 5:15-21. Ask your
Heavenly Father to refresh you
with His truth.

I'm on the road a lot. I love teaching about God's love and how He longs to share a deep and meaningful relationship with each of His children. After a weekend with the girls, it's the sweetest thing to get in my packed-up car and head home. I get a rush every single time I plug in my GPS and hit the icon, "GO HOME." No matter how awesome the time away, I always get excited about getting back to the comforts of home. My husband, who knows and loves me, is on the lookout and always makes getting back home special. My favorite pillow, my man, and my stuff make home warm and inviting.

Think of a time you felt excited about returning home. What comforts and pleasures were you looking forward to experiencing?

Jesus is inviting you back

I've been invited back to my spiritual home, the cross. The Spirit delivered this subtle yet distinct invitation straight to my heart during a late afternoon walk on a balmy spring day. Gently, the message emerged: *You will discover intimacy with Me to the degree you understand My suffering on the cross.*

I remember being hit with a burst of joy the moment I realized I'd heard from God. The next moment brought sheer panic at what these words might mean. A dichotomy began brewing in my spirit. Did I want deeper intimacy or not? Was I willing to experience it by understanding more about suffering, His suffering?

Have you ever really wanted to go deeper with God but were afraid? ◯ yes ◯ no

Circle the areas where love and fear seem to collide.

relationships	finances	future	job	marriage
children	dying	sickness	friendships	faith
other _____				

It's such a delightful experience inviting God to speak to you and recognizing His voice when He does speak. In continuing pleas from my heart, I had often asked Him to show me how to love Him more and to draw me deeper into His presence. Ultimately, love and trust won out over fear in this latest message to my heart. Trusting Him completely, I knew there was absolutely nothing to be afraid of. I also knew that His love was the key that would unlock my heart, freeing me to love Him even more.

> He made the One who did not know sin to be sin for us, so that we might become the righteousness of God in Him.
> 2 Corinthians 5:21

Especially, I knew God was calling me back to the cross. He wanted me to see His outpouring of love as He carried it and then willingly climbed upon it. The suffering He'd endured by voluntarily taking on the sins of the entire world, He endured for me. Jesus, the one Person who had never committed a single sin became sin so that I could receive righteousness!

I knew this. I'd learned it as a small child, but I'd never learned to live in the daily excitement and realization of this holy reality. I had taken it all for granted. Not deliberately but out of ignorance. I simply had never become preoccupied with the cross. Love and relationship were birthed at the cross. That's where home was, and I was headed back there.

Place an X on the line indicating to what degree you think about the cross.

never   continually

All of a sudden, I began to get it. My heart began to melt with a new awareness of the cross and what it meant for me personally. My mind drifted back to my childhood when I first began to be drawn into His presence.

I remembered childhood days of feeling especially joyful playing in the sunshine on late autumn afternoons. I also remembered snuggling up in a blanket and feeling mysteriously drawn into the splattering of raindrops on my bedroom window. As a child, I felt soothed and comforted as I wrapped my arms around my favorite teddy bear at night. I didn't recognize these feelings as belonging to God, but I now know they were straight from His heart. Each time I stood fascinated by a gurgling creek or drank in the warmth of sunshine, He was gently pulling me close. Every time I experienced unexplainable comfort, His Spirit had attracted me to His presence.

Close your eyes and think of a time when God drew you into His presence. Briefly share your experience.

because of the cross, relationship is possible

Years after I'd first experienced these wooings from God's heart, I made a public declaration on a Sunday evening at First Baptist Church in Kings Mountain, North Carolina. I was 12 years old and declared my love for Jesus in front of my family and friends that night. I knew He had died on the cross for me and had forgiven me for all my sins—past, present, and future. I publicly invited Him to live in my heart, asking Him to help me be the person He wanted me to be. As a child, it felt so good to know the truth about Jesus. Not that I understood it, but I did believe it! Jesus and I were at home together in my heart. At the moment I invited Him into my life as my personal Savior, the relationship began. He'd initiated it the day He died on the cross for me.

Check the statements below that apply to you.
- ○ I have deliberately entered into a relationship with Jesus.
- ○ I have never entered into a relationship with Jesus but would like to.
- ○ I feel unsure about whether or not I have a relationship with Jesus.
- ○ I know Jesus lives in my heart, but I do not feel "at home" with Him right now.
- ○ I long to grow deeper in my love relationship with Jesus.
- ○ I want to go back home to the cross and rediscover the freshness of God's love.

Dear Sister, I invite you to journey to the cross with me. If you're not certain that you have invited Jesus Christ into your heart as your personal Lord and Savior, I'm excited for you! Page 133 will give you guidelines about accepting the salvation that Jesus already purchased for you at the cross. Or perhaps He already lives in your heart, but you'd like to refresh your relationship with Him. Here's what I'm discovering: you can't ever step beyond Him. If you keep moving, He longs to take you a step further, then further, and further. It's totally up to you!

As you close today's study, talk to Him about what He did personally for you at the cross.

Worship with this week's hymn, and scribble your thoughts.

Dear Father, thank You for sending Your one and only Son, Jesus, to die on the cross for my sins so that I may enter into a love relationship with You. Please give me new and deeper insights about what Jesus did for me. Draw me deeper into Your love so that each day will be fresh and full of adventure with You. I love You.

day 2 : shifting your gaze

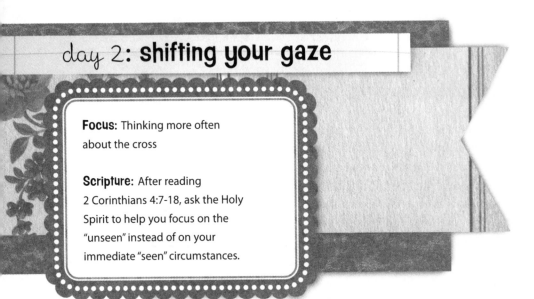

Focus: Thinking more often about the cross

Scripture: After reading 2 Corinthians 4:7-18, ask the Holy Spirit to help you focus on the "unseen" instead of on your immediate "seen" circumstances.

God's personal invitation to me to go deeper with Him hinged on a greater appreciation of the cross. He'd made that crystal clear. For me the cross had been the unseen and unthought of power that made victorious living possible. I knew about the power of the cross in theory but had never practiced an ongoing mindfulness of this most glorious of all truths.

The beginning days of shifting my spiritual eyes to gaze upon the cross brought many tears. I just couldn't believe that I'd lived most of my life being so passionless about what Jesus did for me. It's the most important message in all of history, and yet I'd lived most of my life without giving it much attention. That was about to change! I asked the Lord to show me how to center my thinking on the cross.

center \ *verb* : focus on, revolve around, direct one's attention to something

Circle the areas below that indicate where you have ever centered your thinking.

career	computer	time	husband	exercise
hobbies	education	travel	ministry	children
sports	TV	church	other _____	

back to basics

When you love the Lord and interact with Him daily, He fortifies your heart and mind to receive new insights from Him—and that's sweet (and sometimes funny). He'd begun preparing my heart a month earlier at a Sunday evening worship service at my church. We'd sung a couple of the old songs. I blush now, thinking back to my reaction to those songs with the antiquated tempos and lyrics: *I wish we'd keep the music up to date on Sunday nights. The contemporary music we sing in the mornings is so much more worshipful.*

Weeks later, as God brought that particular Sunday evening to mind, He nudged me to take a look at the old hymnal my parents had given me. As I pulled it from the bookshelf and opened the pages, tears streaked my face. I turned to the first song I'd learned to play on the piano, "At Calvary."

I saw myself, a small 5-year-old, seated beside my grandmother at the old piano that now rests in my home. She patiently stretched my little fingers across the keys and taught me to play and sing the song that now—50 years later—is having an even greater impact on my life. As my eyes scanned the words to that old, familiar hymn, a freshness gave life to the musty smell hovering over that aged hymnal. Unexplainable joy bursted within my heart as I read these words. It seemed I was seeing them for the first time.

> *Years I spent in vanity and pride,*
> *Caring not my Lord was crucified,*
> *Knowing not it was for me He died*
> *On Calvary.*
>
> *Mercy there was great, and grace was free;*
> *Pardon there was multiplied to me;*
> *There my burdened soul found liberty,*
> *At Calvary.*

Have you ever felt like you were seeing something wonderful for the first time?
○ **yes**   ○ **no**

If so, describe.

As I embraced the message of this great old hymn, the phrase "Caring not my Lord was crucified," slowly inched its way into the crevices of my heart. I was at once thrilled and heartbroken. Thrilled because of my newly-realized discovery. Heartbroken that it seemed to describe me.

So many years of knowing and loving Jesus, yet never really *caring* about what He had done for me. I knew about it but had not cared. Caring, in the sense of thanking Him and giving serious attention to the cross daily, had not been of paramount importance to me. I was suddenly so ashamed at such a grievous offense. The guilt weaseled in.

grace!

It's important to let you know that during that moment of conviction, a deluge of God's grace drenched me. Immediately He seemed to say, "Yesterday was an important part of today's journey. Continue now with opened eyes and opened heart to see and receive all that is yours." Ahh, the sweet grace of our Lord; grace that exceeds our sin and our guilt.

Are you nursing shame and guilt in your life? ○ yes ○ no

If so, circle the phrases that describe what you long to experience.

rest	lightheartedness	freedom from guilt
joy	forgiveness	renewed purpose for living
peace	restored relationship	other _____

My friend, freedom to get out from under those cumbersome burdens is yours for the asking. Freedom to experience newfound joy and adventure is totally possible. How is this true? Because:

> *Mercy there was great, and grace was free;*
> *Pardon there was multiplied to me;*
> *There my burdened soul found liberty,*
> *At Calvary.*

If you are dismissing the cross as the center of your life, then you're probably monitoring your relationship with God on your changing emotions. Or maybe you're measuring your daily walk by your performance. Perhaps you're even more attuned to your past or present sins, living with guilt and shame. If so, you're not living in the freedom won for you at Calvary.

When you begin to focus on the unseen cross rather than your seen circumstances, you'll begin to taste and then savor the glorious freedom won for you by your Lord Jesus Christ.

This marvelous grace! You don't have to pay for it, work for it, or perform to get it. It's yours for the taking. While this grace comes to you freely, it cost the Savior His life.

As you leave today's study, will you choose to bring His cross clearly into focus? Will you joyfully embrace it and allow the reality of His grace to take up residence in your heart and emotions?

Worship with this week's hymn, and scribble your thoughts.

> So we do not focus on what is seen, but on what is unseen. For what is seen is temporary, but what is unseen is eternal. 2 Corinthians 4:18

Dear Jesus, I long to live in the freedom You won for me on the cross. I thank You with all of my heart for the price You paid so that I could share daily life with You. Forgive me for taking it all for granted. I'm coming back home to the cross. When life gets tough and the stressors pile up, teach me how to focus on Your unseen grace. I love You.

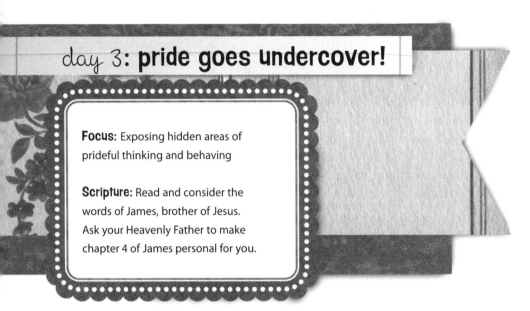

day 3: **pride goes undercover!**

Focus: Exposing hidden areas of prideful thinking and behaving

Scripture: Read and consider the words of James, brother of Jesus. Ask your Heavenly Father to make chapter 4 of James personal for you.

During the months following God's revelation, He continued to draw my attention to the cross and what His death meant to me personally. Meanwhile, He focused my attention on another phrase in that great hymn, "At Calvary." It was a phrase that led to deep examination and introspection.

"Years I spent in vanity and pride." There it was; highlighted it seemed, just for me. I was pretty sure this condition of pride was lurking in some unsuspected places in my thoughts and behaviors. Being drawn to this phrase led me straight to Scripture to find out exactly what God's Word had to say about it all. Honestly, I became expectant, wondering if He would show me areas where pride had taken up residence in my own heart. Well, He sure did!

cravings at war

"What is the source of wars and fights among you? Don't they come from the cravings that are at war within you?" (Jas. 4:1).

I remember some intense cravings as a young mother: cravings to have wonderfully responsible and obedient children who honored their parents, fitting right into the family schematic that I had designed. Yep, those cravings soon produced war within me and within my home.

My friend Amy, who has teenagers and a degree in psychology, talks about how we, as perfectionistic parents, just don't want to get it wrong. It's easy for our children to become our experiment of getting right what went wrong for us.

Hmm. See pride floating around in those scenarios?

When my boys were young I often had to step back from the situation and analyze why I was insisting on things being done just my way. Quite often I traced that why right back to pride. What other people observed in my children said a lot about me, so I had to make sure my reputation was covered. More than seldom, the condition of my ego corresponded to the performance of my kids.

Stay with me here. There are good and appropriate reasons for parents to insist that things be done according to their guidelines. Those are not the areas I'm talking about. Let's consider the other where pride may have crept in, creating war within you and within your family.

Check the areas where you may be a bit heavy on the pride side. In other words, how important is your reputation in these areas?

- ○ how your children dress
- ○ academic achievement
- ○ your children and sports
- ○ your husband's job
- ○ personality (children or husband)

- ○ family's behavior in social settings
- ○ what kind of house you live in
- ○ conduct (children or husband)
- ○ organization on the home front
- ○ other _____

Continuing this self-examination, I asked the Holy Spirit to continue to reveal other areas where pride was keeping me absorbed with self. He did.

what about me?

That was the very thought that surfaced when another speaker was chosen for the women's event for which I just knew I was best suited. (I'm just being transparent here. In order to address this issue within ourselves and with each other, we must take a soulful look at the responses and motives of our hearts.) I gradually began to see that what I had earlier viewed as just an acceptable response to the disappointment of not being chosen as the keynote speaker was nothing other than pride.

And what about last week when I felt I wasn't appreciated enough for cooking and cleaning when I really needed to be investing my time elsewhere, like "doing things for Jesus"? OK, rolling with the transparency again.

now it's your turn

Did you have any "What about me" thoughts last week? ○ yes ○ no

If so, in what areas were they screaming? Circle all that apply.

caregiving	family	friendships
cooking	cleaning	ministering
volunteering	neighborhood things	organizing the home front
leisure time	running errands	taxiing
on-the-job	church activities	other_____

My friend, are you willing to admit that these places where you feel overlooked, underappreciated, and not even considered are actually areas of prideful thinking? If you can begin to do that, you are stepping up for some huge blessings from the heart of God. Going there may be strangely difficult at first. The Enemy wants to disguise this area of pride. That's what he does best. He's the great deceiver, coaxing you into believing you have the right to feel this way or that.

He disguises pride in such a way that you don't even realize its existence. You simply pass it off as taking care of Number One or perhaps getting your needs met in a healthy way. After all, don't we all need a little "Attagirl!" for pouring our energies into the lives of others?

So, is it really pride? Let's take a look.

pride \ *noun* : a high or inordinate opinion of one's own dignity, importance, merit, or superiority

Yep, that definition of pride seems to pretty much encapsulate what's going on in my thinking when I'm overlooked, not chosen, not thanked, or not particularly noticed. That definition is also a fit for the times I link my self-esteem to what others think of my family.

Now in case you need some help to connect prideful thinking with embracing the cross, let me remind you that our Savior never shouted "What about Me?" as He hung there on the cross for us. He selflessly gave everything He was and everything He had so we could live in freedom from sin's trap of self-indulgence. Why is it a trap? Because being bound up in self keeps your attention and affections focused on you instead of on Jesus.

We've stepped into a touchy area today. It's never easy to address this issue of pride. The Enemy has much success in keeping us blinded and unwilling to even address pride's presence. As you close today's study time, will you prayerfully consider thoughts and behaviors in your lifestyle that have pride at the root?

Worship with this week's hymn, and scribble your thoughts.

Dear Father, please help me to reexamine my thinking in light of Your Word. Reveal to me any prideful thoughts that are creating war within my heart and strife within my family. Help me to view myself and others through Your eyes of love. Thank You for loving me. I love You.

Focus: Growing in humility

Scripture: Once again, read James 4. Prayerfully ask your Heavenly Father to reveal areas of prideful thinking.

self's importance

Pride and vanity lead to a self-absorbing lifestyle. Being consumed with self soaks up your time and energy. I cringe thinking about the moments I've wasted being consumed with me: how I look, how I feel, what others think about me.

It's a mad roller-coaster ride of highs and lows, with me being at the mercy of the twists and turns as I'm seated strapped in with the vanity bar holding me in place. I inch upward, stall a few seconds before getting hurled full-speed downward, looping around and twirling upside down. The momentary peace I feel between those twists and turns is quickly disrupted when I began to obsess again about how I look, what they think, has anyone noticed me?

Can you identify? Before we beat ourselves up over our egocentric attitudes, let me point out we've had plenty of help getting where we are today. We live in a society consumed with self. There's a draw to many products and services aimed at improving self. Self-help books, self-help seminars, and self-help mental and physical training programs abound, along with self-help infomercials and self-help eating regimens. Although not necessarily harmful, this tendency to place so much emphasis on self can lead you to lose focus of others.

It's important to consider self but within proper balance.

Circle the areas where you tend to be overly consumed with self.

appearance	performance	recognition from others
talents	abilities	perfectionistic tendencies
behavior	achievements	acceptance from others
intellect	other _____	

It's not that we want to kill all thoughts of self, but we do want to slay those excessive areas of pride. How can that be done? By turning to grace, God's grace. That freely-given, unearned favor of God influences our spirit and operates within us, allowing us to show the same favor toward others as He has shown to us.

humility's importance

James reminds us, "God resists the proud, but gives grace to the humble" (4:6).

I long for God's grace to abound in my life. At times I feverishly yearn to think like Him, feel like Him, and be totally controlled by Him. According to His Word, His grace enters through the door of humility. Oh what a promise! He actually gives grace to those who humble themselves before Him.

If you're longing for more grace to abound in your thinking, then perhaps it would be helpful to run a little vanity and pride antivirus program on your mental computer. Is the home page of your thinking filled with thoughts of grace, living in freedom, enjoying hanging out with God, and enjoying excitement with Jesus?

Or has that unwelcomed intruder moved in and infiltrated your thinking with feelings of self-importance, self-criticism, regrets over your past, shame, and guilt? What about feelings of revenge, retaliation, and a vindictive spirit?

Are you beginning to see how pride and vanity can take root in your heart, causing you to totally dismiss living in God's grace, much less showing it to others?

Check statements below that apply to you much of the time.
- ○ I often worry about what others think about me.
- ○ I'm easily agitated when things don't go my way.
- ○ Even though I know Jesus has forgiven me, I still wrestle with guilt.
- ○ I walk in freedom from my past.
- ○ My self-esteem is often based on how well I handle a situation.
- ○ If someone looks at me and doesn't speak, I worry about it for days.
- ○ I enjoy life with God, unhindered by burdens revolving around self.
- ○ I consider what others think of me but quickly turn these thoughts over to Jesus.

Truthfully, I had never associated concern over what others think about me with being prideful.

This newfound realization came during a Frazzled Female event when a seasoned and committed Christian captured me at break time. We went outside on the deck, and she poured her heart out to me. She'd tried many times over the years but just could not break free of obsessing about what others thought of her. Although she didn't call it pride, we both came to realize that was exactly what it was.

Nanci (we'll call her) is a born-again Christian. Her position of salvation declares that she has died to sin along with Christ and has been raised to new life in Him.

"The death he died, he died to sin once for all; but the life he lives, he lives to God. In the same way, count yourselves dead to sin but alive to God in Christ Jesus" (Rom. 6:10-11, NIV). While I neither understand fully nor can explain the doctrinal theology behind these verses, I can tell you that Nanci was in full-fledged spiritual warfare over the reality of her position in Christ and the mind-set of what the world thinks.

"There is another power within me that is at war with my mind. This power makes me a slave to the sin that is still within me" (Romans 7:23, NLT).

While we live on this earth and in this body, sin is still a part of our nature. But there's coming a day when sin will be totally eradicated in our perfectly redeemed bodies. Woohoo! In the meantime, we recognize its presence and rely on the Holy Spirit to slay the sin that causes us to feel defeated, worthless, and immobile.

Do you sometimes fight in that "people-pleasing war"? Does your heart yearn, like Nanci's, to be freed from the bondage that is keeping your self-esteem tied to what others think of you?

Place an X on the scale to show how much of your self-respect revolves around "what others think." (Be honest. This is transparency between you and God.)

1	2	3	4	5	6	7	8	9	10
not at all									all the time

Do you think being wrapped up in what others think of you qualifies as being filled with vanity and pride? ○ yes ○ no ○ have never thought about it before

pride \ *noun* : a high or inordinate opinion of one's own dignity, importance, merit, or superiority

vanity \ *noun* : excessive pride in one's appearance, qualities, achievements, and so forth

Look again at the definitions of pride and vanity. Are you beginning to see that being so consumed with the opinion of others is placing excessive emphasis on your importance and achievements?

Being the people pleaser that I am, I am learning that becoming excessively wrapped up in what others think of me is being way too consumed with me. Realizing this is helping me shed some prideful issues that have been a huge part of my personal focus.

As you close today's study time, reflect on what has been revealed to you regarding vanity and pride.

Worship with this week's hymn, and scribble your thoughts.

Dear Father, help me to be forgiving to myself as You reveal these areas of pride and vanity to my heart. Thank You for the tremendous freedom that comes from acknowledging and confessing this sin. I long to attract more grace, Lord. I long to humble myself before You so that I can live a life glorifying You. Thank You for Your mercy. Thank You for Your grace. I love You.

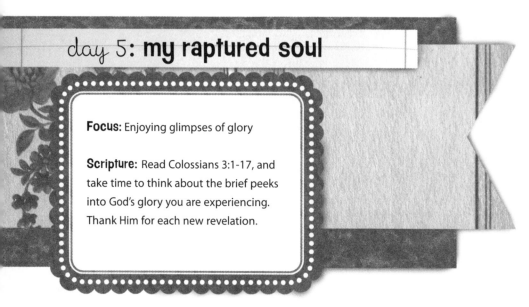

day 5: my raptured soul

Focus: Enjoying glimpses of glory

Scripture: Read Colossians 3:1-17, and take time to think about the brief peeks into God's glory you are experiencing. Thank Him for each new revelation.

rapture \ *noun* : ecstatic joy or delight; joyful ecstasy

When is the last time you were enraptured over your relationship with Jesus?

My dear Friend, shouldn't we live each moment of every day filled with such joy and ecstasy? I long to live daily with a grateful heart for what my Lord did for me and continually does for me. I don't want a single day to pass without pausing to thank Him throughout, reflecting upon His incredible sacrifice of love for me. I ache to live in an ongoing awareness of Him, having a lifestyle of gratitude and wonder.

cut to size

I'm discovering that facing the cross keeps me in that position of thankfulness. When I allow my heart and mind to become cross-absorbed, the importance of self just melts away. I begin trading my self-importance with the glory of Christ. As I inch my way toward becoming consumed with His hugeness, the bigness of me just doesn't matter.

Moving away from self-focus has been very gradual for me; gradual, but real. I'm far from being totally there, but I am making progress. And I can tell you this; it's wonderfully liberating.

Can you also testify of a gradual moving away from self-focus?
○ yes ○ no ○ gradually getting there

Can you identify with the longing of my heart to live in a thankful awareness of His sacrifice on the cross? ○ yes ○ no ○ gradually getting there

Is the "moving away from self-focus" liberating for you? ○ yes ○ no

Explain.

During this time of reflection on the cross, I have become more in tune with His grace.

grace \ *noun* **:** the freely given, unmerited favor and love of God

Focusing on the grace extended to me has opened my heart to opportunities to extend this same favor and love to others. I can tell you this is not a Cindi thing. It's totally God and divinely supernatural. You see, being caught up in the grace of God poured out on the cross absolutely frees me to pour that same grace out to every single person I encounter throughout my day. Each day brings with it a new holy experiment to think, feel, and behave like Jesus. He's prompting me to actively look for ways to offer His grace to others.

Think of the past 24 hours. Circle areas needing a hefty dose of God's grace.

traffic	workplace	phone conversation
home front	store	school
doctor's office	committee meeting	restaurant
bank	other _____	

Will you right now commit to actively look for ways to show God's grace today?
○ yes ○ no ○ not today

If yes, write about your experience after your "grace giving."

celebrating the cross

What does it mean to celebrate the cross? Simply this. When Jesus died on Calvary, He opened the door of relationship. Later in our study, we'll explore some theological terms, but for now just realize that apart from the blood of Christ shed on the cross, you cannot be in relationship with the Heavenly Father. The precious blood of Jesus escorted us right into the Father's arms. And that's cause for celebration.

Now my raptured soul can only sing
Of Calvary!

I'm rejoicing over our baby steps, yours and mine. As I'm nearing the end of this week's study, I'm reflecting on the deep emotions I've experienced in my own heart. I've never been so caught up in the message of the cross as I am now. For the first time, His sacrifice has become deeply personal to me. As I've reflected on each Scripture and sung the lyrics to the great old hymns accompanying this study, I've been brought to my knees time and time again. And with each one, there's opportunity to glorify God.

Are you having the same experience?   ○ yes   ○ no

If yes, explain.

Colossians 3:2 says, "Set your minds on what is above, not on what is on the earth." Each time we manage to set our mind on the above, we welcome the opportunity to experience great joy. I'm talking about practical, everyday opportunities.

Listen. We have a real God who has real answers for daily living.

If He had not come through for me so many times in practical daily ways, I wouldn't be writing about it. When you set your mind on what is above, junkie things happening on earth don't tilt you over the edge. Like, yesterday …

In the midst of my running and doing and marking off my list, all of a sudden I realized I was famished. I ran by my favorite fast-food place and ordered my favorite fast-food sandwich and received my not-at-all-what-I-ordered-meal. As my fleshly spirit riled up, grace settled me down. I truly enjoyed the sweet opportunity of looking into the face of the server who knew she'd gotten it all wrong. Grace spilled out of my mouth instead of agitation. Grace opened the door of relationship to this dear girl for a few moments. Those same moments could have ruined her day and mine too. I couldn't even eat the sandwich, but it didn't matter. God's grace filled me up. Don't know how that happened, but I know it did.

Don't be fooled into thinking incidents like these are trivial. These kinds of events make up all of life. One after the other.

Think of a possible source of agitation in your day ahead. Imagine grace taking over. Do you think you could alter the possible outcome by extending some grace? Explain.

Do you see that each time you extend grace to another, you seize that opportunity to produce the fruit of humility in your own spirit? Do you see that joy and humility walk hand in hand? Explain.

You don't become enraptured with Jesus by trying harder. You become enraptured with Him by loving Him, thanking Him, and becoming more like Him in your dealings with others

Take a moment to prayerfully sing as you wrap up week 2.

Now, I've given to Jesus everything,
Now I gladly own Him as my King;
Now my raptured soul can only sing
Of Calvary.

Worship with this week's hymn, and scribble your thoughts.

Dear Savior, Thank You for the cross. Thank You for fresh revelations about Your love. Open my heart and my mind to the truth about Your grace. Help me find ways every single day to offer Your love to those around me. I love You.

There Is Power in the Blood

Would you be free from the burden of sin?

There's power in the blood, power in the blood;

Would you over evil a victory win?

There's wonderful power in the blood.

Would you do service for Jesus your King?

There's power in the blood, power in the blood;

Would you live daily His praises to sing?

There's wonderful power in the blood.

There is power, power, wonder-working power

In the blood, of the Lamb;

There is power, power, wonder-working power

In the precious blood of the Lamb.

—Lewis E. Jones, 1899

3

His blood, my transfusion

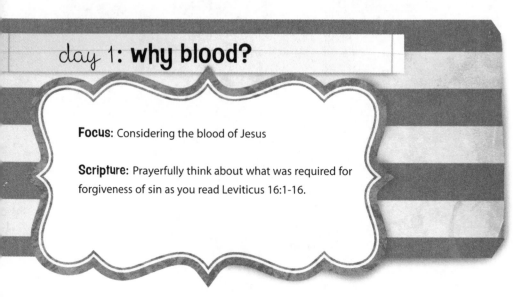

day 1: **why blood?**

Focus: Considering the blood of Jesus

Scripture: Prayerfully think about what was required for forgiveness of sin as you read Leviticus 16:1-16.

two questions

I'd like for you to mull over the following questions for several moments.

Are you teaching "the blood"? What does "covered in the blood of Jesus" mean?

My Uncle Sonny, a strong follower of this ministry, posed the first question to me. The second came from a devoted Christian, searching for more spiritual depth in his personal relationship with Jesus.

Next, pretend you're back in middle school. You're a 12-year-old who has just been given a creative writing assignment. Your instructions are to brainstorm every word and picture that comes to your mind when you hear the word *blood*. Ready, set, go for it! You have 60 seconds.

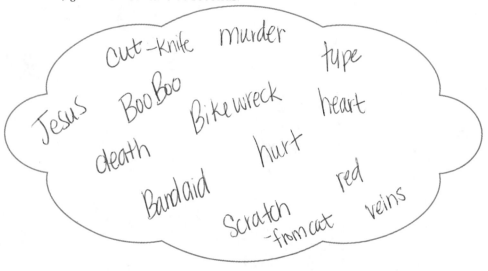

How'd you do? Did you come up with some gross words and images? (I love how kids think!) Keeping this content honest and teachable, I must confess to you that even as a mature Christian (in years, that is) my theological understanding of "the blood" for most of my life has been pretty much in line with that of a sixth grader. I rarely gave serious thought to Christ's blood. Even while singing, "There is power, power, wonder-working power in the precious blood of the Lamb," I seldom entered into that awesome power.

How about you? Beyond acknowledg_____ _____ ___ial shedding of Christ's blood during the Easter season, do you regu____ _____ ___lue of His most precious gift to you?

(I'm resisting the urge to have you _____ _____ ____ten you think about the blood of Jesus. If you're _

beyond the comfort zon_

Perhaps you're like I once was____ _____ _____ came across as archaic and even at times, dis____ _____ _____k understanding of their meaning, I was pretty ____ _____ ___ese phrases conjured up. The word *blood* to me ___ ____ _____ __lication to my daily Christian life. In my thinki___ ___ ____ _____ much reserved for those who were not necessarily ___ ____ ___ were "different" than I was in their worship o___ ___ ____ __e blood" were absent from my daily spiritual ___ _____ __scious awareness of their relevance to my positi___

As a Christian, circle ___ ____ ___ever considered distasteful or **simply dismissed a**___ ___ ____ ____ionship with God.
   pleading the blo___ ___ **bought by the blood**
   sprinkling the ___ ___ **benefits of the blood**
   saved by the ___ ___ **protected by the blood**
   other _____

I'm not ass___ ____ ___ ___is study have had the same experience as mine. I ___ ___ ___ward to make sure we progress from this point ___ ___ ____ of the importance and the relevance of Christ's she___ ___ ___dren.

The Old Testament _ ___ ___ __e word *blood* and thought *life*. Many New Testament Christians hear the w___ __ood and think *death*. The Old Testament Hebrew thought *precious*. Many New Testament Christians think *yucky*. Those living under the Old Covenant understood that the term "covered in the blood" meant life and forgiveness of sin through the sacrificial procedure.

In the sacrificial system they understood that they were guilty and that they could not, on their own merits, approach God. They knew that because of God's perfection and ultimate judgment, they could not even worship Him due to their own impurity. Their guilt needed to be "paid for." This payment for their sinful imperfection took the form of a "blood sacrifice" (meaning a "life sacrifice"). The best they had—the most perfect lamb, ram, bull, whatever—they took to the altar. The priest would kill the animal, allowing its blood to drip over the altar, symbolizing that their sin-debt, for the time being, had been covered by the blood.

Yes, they were definitely at home with this practice and all the conversation surrounding it. Their Facebook status read, "My family is right with God today, thanks to the precious blood of our sacrificial lamb!"

pause

Stop! Put down this book and pick up God's Word. Read Leviticus 4. Take your time. Even if you don't finish today's lesson, do not rush through and dismiss the importance of God's requirement for the forgiveness of sin.

After reading and contemplating God's Word in Leviticus 4, check the following statements that express your thoughts at this moment.
- ○ **I don't even know what I just read.**
- ☑ **God gave such complicated instructions.**
- ○ **How could a common, ordinary person approach God?**
- ○ **Why was it so hard to please God?**
- ○ **Other** _____

My friend, I've been poring over these passages for some time now, and I still don't get it. It's all very complicated and hard to follow, even with the Scriptures describing the steps of the system God set up for His people through Moses.

Thankfully, we don't have to understand it all. That Old Covenant system has been done away with by the sacrifice of Jesus our Lord. On the cross, He paid the debt and fulfilled the impossible requirements of God. God initiated this course of reconciliation with fallen humanity because He loves us and desires relationship with all those He created.

I am convinced of this: for any who want to grow deeper in love with Jesus, it's critical to look deeply into the meaning of His shed blood. Being in relationship with Jesus Christ means you are blood-bought and blood-covered. If your desire for Him is growing and you want to plumb the depths in this relationship, let's hold spiritual hands and inch our way closer to the cross. Together we'll explore the glorious truth about His blood.

Worship with this week's hymn, and scribble your thoughts.

Dear Heavenly Father, I ask that You excite my heart to the possibilities ahead for our love relationship. I feel pretty ignorant right now, reading these Old Testament passages describing the steps to approaching You. Give me understanding into what You want me to know so that I can more deeply appreciate the sacrifice of Jesus. Open my mind and heart to "blood talk" so that I can adequately praise You for the most precious of all gifts—Your blood. Amen.

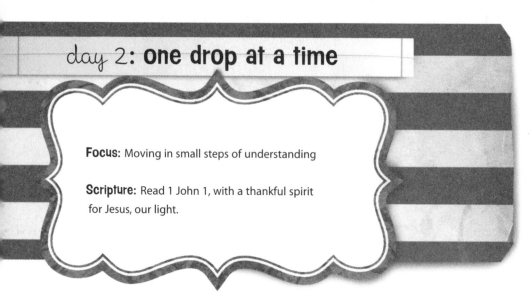

day 2: **one drop at a time**

Focus: Moving in small steps of understanding

Scripture: Read 1 John 1, with a thankful spirit for Jesus, our light.

inching forward

Yesterday we contemplated the blood of Jesus and what His blood did for us personally. By deepening our understanding of the Old Testament sacrificial system, we begin to realize the power in the imagery of Jesus as the Lamb of God, the ultimate and eternal sacrifice made once for all. Just as the blood of the sacrificial animal covered the altar—thus covering the sins of the people—the blood of Jesus covers us and our sins. It's being "legally" put right, "paid off" so that we can enter into a restored relationship with God. Yes, we've truly been bought by the blood of Jesus.

Think of it like this: You loaned me $50 last month and I still haven't paid you back. So you keep fussing about my debt. My good friend doesn't like hearing you fuss about the $50, neither does she like seeing me owe something she knows I cannot pay. So she takes off her favorite gold bracelet and hands it to you saying, "This will cover her debt." I did not pay what I owed; my friend paid it for me. She "covered" my debt with her gold bracelet. Take note that the debt I owed didn't just disappear. It was paid by one who loves me.

I have a sin debt. The sacrifice of Jesus Christ (shedding of blood) paid my sin debt. That debt did not simply disappear. No. The debt I owed was paid by One who loves me.

When we say phrases such as "covered in the blood," "bought by the blood," and "protected by the blood," we could as easily say, "covered in His sacrifice," "bought by His sacrifice," and "protected by His sacrifice." It's synonymous. It may be more comfortable for you to think in those terms. However, let me offer this thought. According to Revelation 12:11, the saints in heaven "conquered [the Devil] by the blood of the Lamb and by the word of their testimony." These believers depended on Christ's blood and their spoken testimony about Jesus to overcome the Enemy and their fear of death. In the same way, we can call upon the blood of Jesus through our spoken word to stand against all the tactics of the Enemy.

I've included the previous explanations and verses to help you process your thoughts regarding the sacrifice of Jesus and the verbiage surrounding His blood.

Making any headway in your understanding? Place an X on the graph, charting your progress.

not getting it	gradually understanding	figured out

"Applying the blood" with understanding, reverence, and awareness of meaning is a powerful spiritual weapon. My understanding combined with faith releases God's power in the situation I am facing. Personally, I now regularly claim the full provision of Jesus' shed blood on behalf of my family and friends, along with situations I am facing. All along, I'm very aware that the power is not me; it's in me!

Remember the question from my Uncle Sonny? "Are you teaching the blood?"

I've since realized his interest and deep prayer for my ministry. Uncle Sonny knew I realized my highest calling was loving Jesus and, from this love, guiding others to deepen their personal love for our Lord. He also knew that this level of depth in my relationship with Jesus could only happen by going back to His sacrifice on the cross and giving intentional thought to the life and blood He so willingly gave up for me.

Oh, what a journey filled with adventure! I'm experiencing increased joy and passion as I research these truths. We are exploring the very heart of God when we turn our attention to the cross and the sacrifice of His dear Son. It must surely delight Him when we mine the riches of His love.

What are your thoughts regarding God's pleasure at our cross quest?

Can you think of Scriptures to back up your thoughts? If so, list them here.

benefits for His children

Turn to the following Scriptures and fill in the blanks.

Because of His Blood ...
1. I have redemption through His _Blood_ , according to the riches of His grace (see Eph. 1:7).
2. I have been declared _Justified_ (see Rom. 5:9).
3. My conscience and mind have been _purged_ from sin (see Heb. 9:14).
4. I am at _peace_ with God through my Lord Jesus Christ (see Rom. 5:1).
5. I can boldly approach _the holiest_ without fear (see Heb. 10:19).

When you genuinely and reverently ask your Heavenly Father to make the message of Christ's shed blood meaningful to you, He does. When you, by faith, search for deeper revelation, you'll have your spiritual eyes opened. And when you become secure in your knowledge of the cleansing and justifying power of His blood, you will experience all of life differently. The Holy Spirit will begin to breathe new life into old and familiar Scripture passages and hymns. You'll move into a whole new level of your love relationship with Him.

remember this

Even though you may not hear a lot of teaching about blood, the Scriptures are full of references to it. Blood is woven throughout the entire Bible. Sacrifices in the Old Testament were drenched in blood. The New Testament records the ultimate sacrifice in the blood of Jesus Christ. Without the shedding of His blood, there's no chance of approaching God, no hope of salvation, and no assurance that our prayers are even heard. How could we ever so easily dismiss what God's Word regards as vitally important?

Place a check by the sentences that echo your thinking right now.
○ Before this study, I'd never thought a lot about the blood of Jesus.
○ Sometimes, thinking about His bloodshed is too sad and intense for me.
○ I want to understand what the blood of Jesus has to do with experiencing daily victory.
○ Since God considers sacrificial blood important, I will no longer disregard it.
○ I want to understand and accept the provisions of His blood for me and for my family.

let's review

In teaching school, I found that academic progress went hand in hand with much review. Since I love this topic so much and I do believe it pleases God for us to spend time here, bear with me as I offer the following review. Enjoy letting the truth sink way down deep inside your heart.

The sacrificial routine established by God taught the Israelites that He was holy and that transgressions had to be punished. By God's design, the seriousness of sin was dealt with through the slaughter and blood of innocent animals. The Old Testament word *atonement* means *covering*. To cover transgressions, the animals chosen for sacrifice had to be perfectly unblemished. Through this procedure, God taught that the penalty for sin is death and that the penalty must be paid for by the guilty one or an acceptable substitute. By God's decree, atonement for sin was only possible through the shedding of innocent blood. Every animal sacrifice on the altar was a fulfillment of the death penalty required by God.

Worship with this week's hymn, and scribble your thoughts.

Dear Heavenly Father, thank You for Your great love and patience with me as I inch closer to the cross. I'm excited Lord, thinking that my journey is pleasing to You. Keep me at it; learning, growing, delighting in each new revelation that comes from Your heart to mine. I love You.

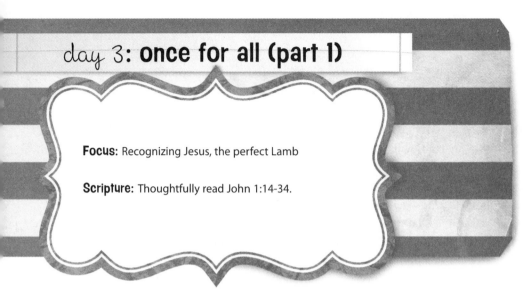

day 3: once for all (part 1)

Focus: Recognizing Jesus, the perfect Lamb

Scripture: Thoughtfully read John 1:14-34.

Regarding the animal sacrifice during Old Testament times, the animal's blood did not take away sins, only covered them. That's why the same procedure was repeated over and over. There were always new sacrifices; there was always new blood to cover the ongoing sin nature of humanity. Can't you just imagine that as the time of each sacrifice drew near the Israelites longed once again to move into that state of forgiveness? What a burden it must have been carrying those sins around, waiting until the next sacrifice to once again be at peace with God.

Hebrews 10:3-4 says, "In the sacrifices there is a reminder of sins every year. For it is impossible for the blood of bulls and goats to take away sins."

Fill in the blanks below from the material we've covered so far in week 3.
God established the sacrificial system to teach that transgressions had
to be ___forgivin___.
The seriousness of ___sins___ was dealt with through the blood of innocent animals.
The animal chosen for the sacrifice had to be perfectly ___Flawless___.
The sacrifice was ___repeated___ over and over.
The Old Testament word *atonement* meant ___Covering___.
The animal's sacrifice did not ___take___ ___away___ sins, only covered them.

Jesus, the perfect lamb and the perfect sacrifice

As Jesus strolled toward John the Baptist alongside the Jordan River, John recognized the mission of Jesus. "Here is the Lamb of God, who takes away the sin of the world!" (John 1:29).

You see, the system of sacrificing blood to cover sin was a foreshadowing of the ultimate and final sacrifice on the cross. Jesus, not merely a man but the Son of God, entered right smack-dab into the middle of sinful humanity to carry out God's awesome plan to save mankind by the shedding of His own blood. As 1 Peter 1:18-19 says, "You know that you were redeemed from your empty way of life ... not with perishable things ... but with the precious blood of Christ."

By becoming the perfect sacrifice, Jesus annulled the Old Testament sacrificial system. Now, for the first time ever and forever more, sin would not merely be covered but would be taken away. He was the *spotless* lamb because His birth was supernatural. There was no sin transferred by a human father, since He was conceived by the Holy Spirit. His life was flawless and therefore the only suitable sacrifice for the sin of all mankind.

Beside each statement place *O.T.* for Old Testament sacrifice or *J* for Jesus' sacrifice.

____ The atonement for sin was repeated over and over.

____ Individuals could not approach the holy place.

____ Sin was removed once and for all.

____ This system was flawed and carried out by man.

____ Because of this sacrifice I am welcomed in God's presence.

____ This sacrifice was perfect.

____ The burden of sin hangs over until the next sacrifice.

____ I am freed from the burden of sin.

the burden of sin has been removed!

Pause in praise and worship as you sing this great old hymn.

pause

Would you be free from the burden of sin?
There's power in the blood, power in the blood;
Would you over evil a victory win?
There's wonderful power in the blood;
There is power, power, wonder-working power
In the blood of the Lamb.
There is power, power, wonder-working power
in the precious blood of the Lamb.

Tell me, my friend. Do you long to walk in glorious freedom from every useless encumbrance that weighs down your soul? You can! If you have received the life-giving sacrifice of Jesus Christ, then He has truly freed you from every sin and all the shame that accompanies each one. You may be thinking *I know I'm forgiven, but I still feel guilty.*

Go ahead now—get excited! Through the Holy Spirit's guidance, I'm going to help you get through this. If Jesus lives in your heart, then you certainly need to walk in the glorious freedom that is yours in Christ. You have been truly set free—not only from sin but from the *burden* of sin.

Consider the Guilt Monster.

guilt \ *noun* **:** remorse or self-reproach by feeling that one is responsible for a wrong or offense

Have you ever experienced guilt? ✓ yes   ○ no

If yes, to what degree? Mark with an X on the graph below.

slight   intense   o̶verwhelming

straight to the muscle

I recently had a welcomed experience that perfectly illustrates the freedom that comes with release. Being on the road a lot and at the computer more than that, my neck and shoulder muscles often feel like bedrock held in a vise. When a friend offered a complimentary massage from a spa that opened in our hometown, my gnarled little neck and shoulder sidekicks shouted, "Take it!" Seriously? Someone else paying for me to get all freed up? I'm in.

Targeting the source of discomfort was no problem. My trained masseuse, with her needlelike thumbs, dove straight into the two muscles that had become the home of my pain. The first muscle immediately released. It was as if that vise had been stripped causing the muscle to hang loose and settle into a restful state. I was amazed that I was freed so quickly from the pain that had been my partner for way too long.

It was a while before the second muscle followed suit. In fact, it seemed to have taken a mind of its own, refusing to cooperate with any effort coaxing it into relaxation. It took more than 20 minutes of kneading and cajoling for that stubborn muscle to loosen its taut nerves and knotted tendons.

Before going any further, let's check your muscle status. Are you experiencing any muscle discomfort right now? ○ yes   ○ no

Place an X by the face which most accurately depicts how you're feeling.

If you were offered a no-cost, no-strings-attached treatment that was sure to put you in a state of complete muscle relaxation, would you take it?
○ **Yes, I'd jump at the chance.** ○ **No, I'd be skeptical.**

straight to the sin muscle

We've been looking at the Old Testament sacrificial system. The practice of offering the blood of spotless animals was repeated year after year to cover sins. When Jesus came, He literally went to the middle of the sin muscle, and with a heart full of love, He willingly became the only sacrifice acceptable to the Father for the remission of sins. With His sacrificial blood flowing, sin was no longer covered just until the next sacrifice. It was completely removed—a done deal! Sin lost its grasp on humanity and a New Covenant was birthed. Hebrews 10:9 reminds us, "He takes away the first to establish the second."

Yes, Jesus appeared on earth right in the middle of the gnarled and knotty infestation of sin, blasting it forevermore to smithereens and annihilating its vise on humanity. "The death he died, he died to sin once for all" (Rom. 6:10, NIV).

With the Son of God's holy encounter with sin, you have been offered a gift of total release from sin's grip. It's complimentary because someone else paid the price to get you freed-up from sin and the hideous guilt that accompanies it. This someone else is none other than God Himself, clothed in human flesh, "who loves us and has set us free from our sins by His blood" (Rev. 1:5).

Breathe deeply right now and thank the Lord afresh for His indescribable gift. Let this be your focus for today. Scribble your thoughts.

Dear Father, forgive me for not living in the freedom paid for by Your Son's death on the cross. I love You so much and long to experience freedom from every burden of sin. Show me how, Lord.

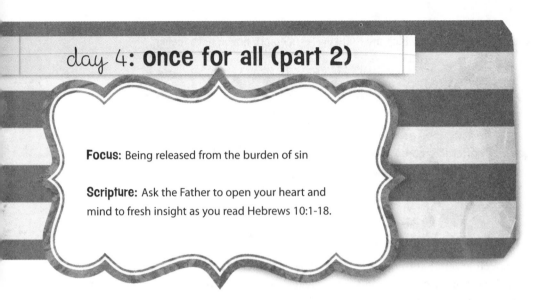

day 4: once for all (part 2)

Focus: Being released from the burden of sin

Scripture: Ask the Father to open your heart and mind to fresh insight as you read Hebrews 10:1-18.

taking it in

As I've saturated my mind and spirit with the depth of His sacrifice, I've been absolutely flabbergasted, if not appalled, at the fact that for much of my life I've not jumped at the chance to live freely. Yes, I'd be quick to tell you I'd been forgiven of my sin—all of it. But in reality, I've lived much of my life as a skeptic. I've sung about the power in the blood without comprehending its significance. I've intellectually accepted the fact of the forgiveness of my sins, but I've not mostly lived in freedom from the burden of it. Seems I just couldn't quite get in the flow of accepting His tremendous sacrifice for what it was—freedom and rest.

Remember that stubborn second muscle I mentioned in day 3? That's me. Even though I know that Jesus has penetrated straight into the mass of sin in my life, there are days I simply refuse to release sin's grip over my soul. My emotions remain knotted and gnarled because I refuse to release them into the heart of God who has given His life so that I may live in the freedom of forgiveness, for which He paid so dearly.

How do you feel about the forgiveness of your sins? Check all that apply.
- ○ I know I've been forgiven.
- ○ Feelings of guilt surface from time to time.
- ○ I don't feel totally "at rest" in the forgiveness of my sins.
- ○ I sometimes try to work harder at "being good" to make up for my sins.
- ○ I want to experience freedom in my mind and emotions, but I don't know how.
- ○ I want to live a thankful life, taking hold of the freedom His sacrifice provides.

recognize the source of unrest

Satan loves to torment God's children. He's drawing you into his trap if you continually allow yourself to dwell on and think about how badly you've messed up. He knows the truth, though—the truth that Jesus came not only to take away your sin but to relieve you from its burden. If you want to walk victoriously with God, then you must accept the freedom that is yours through the removal of sin and the removal of the guilt that accompanies it.

That pesky muscle of mine finally released, moving into rest and relaxation. So can you, but you can't do it on your own. You're not equipped. No amount of determination or self-will will make it happen. You can have victory, however, over the evil schemes of Satan. There's absolutely no reason for a child of God to live under a cloud of guilt. It's not scriptural to do so. The Enemy has been defeated by the blood of Jesus.

You are living in New Covenant times. This Covenant is sealed with Christ's own blood. With the removal of sin, you're free to talk to God and enjoy His presence. A lifestyle of joy, freed from the harassment of sin and its accompanying guilt.

OK. There's His offer, laid out as plainly as I know how. Are you going to jump at it? Freedom is yours—freedom from sin and from sin's burden.

Circle the words that describe one who is experiencing Christ's freedom.

tired	energetic	optimistic	fresh	bogged down
joyful	lifeless	ashamed	weary	lack of purpose
free	restful	peaceful	depressed	filled with hope
burdened	low self-esteem	light and easy living		

pause

Lay down this study and turn your attention to God's Word.
Spend time in Exodus 12:1-14. Let His truth become fresh and personal.
Ask God to speak as you read these verses.

giving up the burden

Exodus 12 will help you understand God's provision for each of His children. Refer to these verses as we explore how His blood can wonderfully change your day-to-day living and free you from the burden of sin.

While the plagues were coming upon the Egyptians, God gave instructions to the Israelites so they could escape this judgment. Fill in the blanks with what God commanded them to do. (See Ex. 12:3-7,13 for help.)

Take an unblemished _____. Kill it and apply some of its

_____to the two _____ and the lintel of the house

where they ate it. The _____on the houses was a distinguishing mark.

Because of the blood, they were not _____.

This Old Testament arrangement was a foreshadowing of the coming of the Messiah, and it has everything to do with you and your position in Jesus Christ today. If Christ is Lord of your life, then His blood has been applied to the doorposts of your heart. A lintel is a horizontal beam over the door. His blood is over you and surrounds you. You have been designated as one of God's own and are kept safe by His blood.

His blood is not only for forgiveness of your sin but for your protection; physically, mentally, and emotionally. There is supernatural power available to God's children because of His shed blood. His blood is life-giving and life-sustaining in the truest sense.

A truth is a verified or indisputable fact. In your own words, write four truths from the content we've covered in our study about the cross.
1.
2.
3.
4.

Is one of these truths particularly stirring your heart? Explain.

action was required

Exodus 12:7 says, "They must take some of the blood and put it on the two doorposts and the lintel of the houses where they eat them."

The previous sentence has two commands. What are they?

They must _____ _____ of the _____.

[They must] _____ it on the two _____and the _____.

A command is an order given by one in authority. In this instance the authority was God. The blood must not be left in the basin. They were instructed to take it and apply it. As long as it was in the basin, it was of no use to them but merely blood that had been shed. Per God's instruction, it had to be applied to stop the destroyer. Action was required, not just belief in the blood.

What do you think would have happened to anyone not following this order to take the blood and apply it? According to Scripture, it would have been doomsday for them, right along with the Egyptians.

Exodus 12:13 promised the Hebrews, "The blood on the houses where you are staying will be a distinguishing mark for you; when I see the blood, I will pass over you. No plague will be among you to destroy you when I strike the land of Egypt."

The Egyptians had no protection from the destroyer. The Hebrews who applied the blood to the doorposts and lintels of their houses were kept safe.

What a revealing passage about the blood of Christ and its provision for our life. One more time: We're living in New Covenant times with Jesus Christ—the Covenant He sealed with His own blood.

Nevertheless, God's solid foundation stands firm, sealed with this inscription: "The Lord knows those who are his" (2 Tim. 2:19, NIV).

deeper and sweeter

Oh, these are deep waters, aren't they? Each rippling of truth beckons us to dive a little deeper and float in His glorious love. How marvelous that our Lord has invited us to life with Him in this New Covenant. How totally awesome the fact that when God looks at me He sees the covering of His Son's blood on my heart. How safe and secure I feel knowing that when the destroyer turns my way, he sees Christ's blood and passes over me. I am protected, sustained, and invigorated by His blood shed for me.

Take a few moments right now to thank God for His glorious blood. Feel free to make the following prayer your own. Scribble your thoughts.

Father, I thank You for the shed blood of Jesus Christ. You've redeemed me and cleansed me from past, present, and future sin. Thank You. You've also taken away the guilt and burden of my sin. Thank You. As I study Your Word throughout these pages, You are bringing me deeper into our relationship. I'm Yours and long to go as deeply as You will allow.

day 5: **power in the blood**

Focus: Remembering what's true

Scripture: Read Hebrews 9:11-28 slowly and thankfully. Ask the Holy Spirit to guide your understanding of these divine truths.

action is required

The only way to enjoy our freedom in this forgiven state is to live in the power of His blood. The only way to serve Jesus Christ is to live in the power of His blood.

How do we do that? First, we must keep mindful of what His blood accomplished for us on the cross. In fact, I've come to the conclusion that dismissing this divine truth is irreverent and nonappreciative.

The Hebrews were instructed to apply the blood to their doorposts. You and I are instructed to apply Christ's blood to our lives (our thinking, behavior, and circumstances). Just as the Israelites were protected from the destroyer, we are protected as we live in full appreciation of the covering of His blood.

pause

Close your eyes right now and visually apply His blood to your day ahead. See yourself reaching out to receive the blood He shed for you on that cross two thousand years ago. Thankfully cover yourself, your family, your concerns, your circumstances, and your joys with His blood. Below list some areas you are covering with His blood.

As I've studied and prayed over the Scripture passages we've explored this week, I've been brought to my knees time and time again. I can't believe how I've missed taking these glorious truths to heart for so many years. I have wept many tears of great joy over these fresh revelations. They've been there all along—right in His Word from the time I held my first little Bible as a child. I just haven't grasped these divine truths as I do now.

There comes a time in each believer's life to move beyond infancy in spiritual matters. There's a time to reach for and chew on the solid food of righteousness. Honestly, I thought I had moved beyond infancy, but in reality I've only been a grown-up babe. Now as never before, I'm hungry for the chunkier truth of God's Word. And the more I taste and chew, the hungrier I become, and the more exciting the journey gets (see Heb. 5:13-14).

As Hebrews 6:1 says, "Let us go on and get past the elementary stage in the teachings and doctrine of Christ the Messiah, advancing steadily toward the completeness and perfection that belong to spiritual maturity" (AMP).

What does the blood of Jesus mean to you personally and practically?

Are you growing in your knowledge of what happened at the cross and your understanding of the worth and value of His shed blood?
○ yes ○ no ○ maybe a little

Do you long for supernatural healing power in a specific area of your life?
○ yes ○ no ○ not now

If yes, explain:

belief and knowledge

The key to unlocking this divine supernatural power in your life lies in your understanding of what His sacrifice accomplished for you on the cross. What you believe about His death and resurrection means everything. Belief and knowledge go and grow hand in hand. If you want to strengthen your ability to believe, then you must increase your knowledge of the facts presented in Scripture.

In other words, you don't believe by trying harder to believe. You believe by having reason to believe. Jesus gave us that reason. In fact, He is the reason. John 5:39-40 says, "These Scriptures are all about me! And here I am, standing right before you, and you aren't willing to receive from me the life you say you want" (Message).

Oh, yes! The Scriptures spread out before you throughout this study are offering life and power. Do you want a life of extraordinary and miraculous power? You'll have it by becoming immersed in Scripture. Do you want to go through your day with new excitement and vitality? Then, engage yourself with God's Word. Increasing your knowledge will strengthen your belief. You don't have to be a theologian or Bible scholar to receive these truths. The only requirement is a hungry heart moving in obedience to receive.

If you desire this new life, then pray the truth found in Jeremiah 29:13, "You will seek Me and find Me when you search for Me with all your heart."

Dear Father, Your Word says when I search for You with my whole heart, I will find You. I want You, Lord. I want all of the power and energy and joy You want to give to me. As I long for You and search for You, I am finding You. Thank You.

what His Word says

We began today's study with a New Testament passage that's married to the Old Testament teachings we've been exploring. Let's ponder the truths found in Hebrews 9:11-28.

The Old Covenant (the former way of doing things) was but a glimmer of glorious things to come.

Christ, our High Priest, has entered heaven—not as the former high priest did with the blood of goats and bulls but with His own blood. Oh, what an age we live in. Such advantages we have in gospel-living as opposed to law-living.

List three advantages you've personally experienced because of living now, instead of Old Testament days.

1.

2.

3.

Pause and thank your Heavenly Father for each advantage.

When Moses presented the blood of goats and bulls for the covering of sin, God accepted it. Likewise, but in greater depth and perfection, when Jesus offered His own blood for our sins, God accepted it. The offering of Christ is the greater sacrifice. His grace has replaced the law of the Old Covenant.

What does this mean for you? Simply this: Jesus Christ, in His one sacrifice, made an end to sin. It is no longer necessary for a high priest to approach God on your behalf. Jesus became your personal and perfect High Priest. With the offering of His blood to God to take away the contamination of your sin, He tore down the wall between heaven and earth, between you and God. You now have free access to God all by yourself. No one has to go before you to approach God for you.

When you enter into relationship with Jesus, accepting the fact that He has indeed covered you and secured you with His own blood, then you are free to approach God with boldness. You're entering His holy presence cloaked in the blood of Jesus Christ.

When He sees you coming, He sees you blanketed in the blood of Jesus, which He accepts. Your sin is not only eclipsed, it is obliterated. You are accepted into God's presence because the blood of Jesus is on you, surrounding you, and covering you. You have no means of accessing and approaching Him apart from the blood of Jesus Christ.

As Hebrews 10:19-21 tells us, "Friends, we can now—without hesitation—walk right up to God, into 'the Holy Place.' Jesus has cleared the way by the blood of his sacrifice, acting as our priest before God. The 'curtain' into God's presence is his body" (Message).

steep your mind and heart in this truth

Are you noticing we're studying from various passages exploring the same glorious truth? This is by God's design. The gospel message is scattered throughout the entire Bible. In thorough examination of a variety of Scriptures all stating the same gospel, your heart and mind become saturated with its infallibility. We must learn to live in daily review and thankfulness if we want to scale the heights with Him. Knowledge and grace grow ever so gradually, but the little growth steps are genuine and awesome. God's blessings are upon us as we inch our way closer to His heart.

James 1:25 reminds us, "If you look carefully into the perfect law that sets you free, and if you do what it says and don't forget what you heard, then God will bless you for doing it" (NLT).

What are four observations from the passage in James 1:25?
1. We must _____ _____ into the perfect law that sets us free.
2. We must _____ what it _____.
3. We must not _____ what we heard.
4. God will _____ us!

The certainty of this Scripture was etched into my heart recently. Charlie, our second grandson, was birthed into our family one week ago as I write. We barely arrived home from our 400-mile trek to welcome him into this world when our son Brandon called. His words touched my heart. "Mom, thank you for all you and dad did when I was born."

Thirteen little words with a lifetime of meaning! For years Brandon understood our love in "present time," but with the birth of his own child, he had a new reference point. For the first time, he considered the sacrifice of love that occurred during the moment of his birth.

My friend, if you're a child of God, the cross is your reference point. It's the place where God proved His love. It's your spiritual birthplace. Who you are today is because of what He did then. I long to continually gaze on the perfect love which set me free, and I long for you to do the same. As we close out week 3, I pray you'll continue to apply these truths to your mind and heart, determining not to forget what you've learned during these days of study. God will rush to bless you. Yes, indeed, He will.

Worship with this week's hymn, and scribble your thoughts.

My Father and Jesus my Savior, thank You for the cross. Gently and genuinely You are revealing Your truths to me. How can I ever thank You enough? Even as that question leaves my lips, I know the answer. The best way to thank You is to give myself to You. Here I am, Lord. I give You me. I walk straight into Your holy presence with all my imperfections and unrighteousness—fully clothed in the blood of Jesus. I humbly and thankfully accept Your glorious gift. I am learning to move freely within Your love and blessings. Thank You, thank You.

Grace Greater than Our Sin

Marvelous grace of our loving Lord,

Grace that exceeds our sin and our guilt,

Yonder on Calvary's mount outpoured,

There where the blood of the Lamb was spilt.

Marvelous, infinite, matchless grace,

Freely bestowed on all who believe;

All who are longing to see His face,

Will you this moment His grace receive?

Grace, grace, God's grace,

Grace that will pardon and cleanse within;

Grace, grace, God's grace,

Grace that is greater

than all our sin.

—Julia H. Johnston, 1910

4

grace?

seriously?

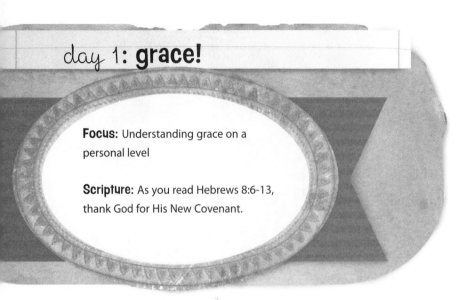

day 1: **grace!**

Focus: Understanding grace on a personal level

Scripture: As you read Hebrews 8:6-13, thank God for His New Covenant.

a new mind-set

Old Covenant law and New Covenant grace are as contrasting as night and day. Taking hold of the new paradigm of grace-living takes a fundamental shift in thinking. As we have learned, Jesus became the mediator of the New Covenant. Because He paid the debt, thus fulfilling the law, the Old Covenant of law was replaced with the New Covenant of grace.

The terms of the New Covenant are not the same as the terms of the Old Covenant. The law required man to work and earn his way to God. Grace says, "Believe and you will receive." Under the law, God related to man through commandments and regulations. Under grace, God relates to us through faith in the shed blood of Jesus Christ.

Write *O* (Old) or *N* (New) beside each statement as it describes either of the Covenants.

__ Sins are remembered.

__ God is fearfully dreaded.

__ Sins are forgotten.

__ God finds fault.

__ God is fearfully honored.

__ God shows mercy.

__ God's law is written on stone tablets.

__ Guilt hangs around until the next sacrifice.

__ God's law is written on man's heart.

__ Routines and rituals are done to appease God.

__ God accepts me through the blood of Jesus.

__ It's impossible to please God.

legalism on the table!

Through study, prayer, and seeking God's thinking about this matter of grace, I've realized that I'm filled up with Old Covenant thinking. Because God has called me to keep this writing transparent and honest, it grieves me to say that much of my Christian life has reeked of legalism—you know, doing things to earn God's approval (and thinking that I could).

For much of my life, I've been a New Covenant gal in an Old Covenant prison.

legalism \ *noun* **:** strict adherence to law, especially to the letter rather than the spirit.
Or theologically speaking, strict adherence to the law rather than His Spirit.

Specifically, I've:
○ signed up for Bible studies to earn God's approval.
○ carried around guilt when I knew I'd been forgiven of sins.
○ tried to please God with church attendance.
○ made phone calls, written notes, and been extra nice, hoping He'd be pleased.
○ offered deals like, "Oh God if You'll _____, I promise to _____."
○ fasted, prayed, memorized Scripture, and completed my devotion—just to appease Him.
○ accepted the lie that He couldn't possibly like and enjoy me.
○ secretly felt like no matter how good I was, He would never approve of me.

OK. My cards are face-up. I need some soul support here. Have you been afflicted with legalistic thinking in any of those areas? If so, place a check beside them above.

How about others?

Take note: Some of those "behaviors and activities" have sprung from a heart of love for the Lord and not out of legalistic thinking. That delights His heart. Look back at the list, underlining those you've also done prompted by love.

Precious Friend, living in ignorance of God's grace is the very thing that keeps many Christians discouraged and weary in their Christian walk. Discouragement is unavoidable when you're trapped in a legalistic mind-set.

Ever had any of these thoughts?

If I would clean up my life, I could ask God for things.	○ yes ○ no
I just need more faith.	○ yes ○ no
I ought to join the ladies' Bible study at church.	○ yes ○ no
I really need to have my quiet time every morning.	○ yes ○ no
I'm such a failure at memorizing Scripture.	○ yes ○ no
I know I need to get back in church.	○ yes ○ no
I think I'll fast to get closer to God.	○ yes ○ no

Give me a couple more.

1.

2.

Here's the basic difference between Old Covenant and New Covenant thinking.

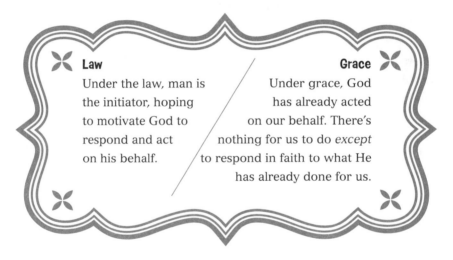

Law

Under the law, man is the initiator, hoping to motivate God to respond and act on his behalf.

Grace

Under grace, God has already acted on our behalf. There's nothing for us to do *except* to respond in faith to what He has already done for us.

Considering those differences, respond to this question: Is your relationship with Jesus Christ mostly characterized by law-living or by grace-living?

In other words, are you the *initiator*, behaving in certain ways and doing certain things that you think will please God so that you can earn His approval? If so, that's Old Covenant thinking. Or are you a *receiver* of grace who says, "I am totally accepted and loved by my Lord. Although I long to please Him, I know I could never earn His love. The things I do for Him are because I love Him and not because I want to gain His favor."

Are you mostly an "initiator" or a "receiver"? Explain your answer below.

bustin' out!

Pardon my slang, but I'm making a dramatic declaration and hoping you'll join me.

By God's grace, I'm breaking out of this Old Covenant death trap. It's a tool of Satan to keep God's children wearily working to earn something that already belongs to them. Don't you see it? If the Enemy can keep you trudging along trying to please God and earn His approval, you'll be totally distracted from living a cross-centered life. Furthermore, not enjoying your inheritance in Christ will keep you from extending God's grace to others around you.

And so goes your world. Havoc surrounds your family, workplace, church, community, and so on, all because you don't understand your position in Christ. That's a strong statement and one that's biblically based.

Hebrews 12:15 says, "See to it that no one misses the grace of God and that no bitter root grows up to cause trouble and defile many" (NIV).

Dear Sister, I am so excited. This can be a life-changing week for you. You've camped out at the cross under His blood, and now you're growing deeper in your understanding of His grace. As I write these words, I'm stopping to lift you to the Father. If you're living in that law death trap, I'm praying that right now you'll determine to bust out!

Oh Father, for me, taking hold of these grace truths has been revolutionary. Now, I pray for my sisters. If there are those striving to earn Your love, please open their spiritual eyes to Your freeing grace. Help them to see the areas in their lives where they're working to earn Your approval. Free them from the Old Covenant mind-set— adhering to the laws written on stone. Reveal to them Your law of love written within their hearts and minds. Take their hearts of stone where they've been living under the law, and refresh them with a new heart of grace. Amen.

As we close today, reflect God's grace in His Word. "I will give you a new heart and put a new spirit within you; I will remove your heart of stone and give you a heart of flesh" (Ezek. 36:26). "This is the covenant that I will make … I will put My laws into their minds and write them on their hearts" (Heb. 8:10).

Worship with this week's hymn, and scribble your thoughts.

Oh Heavenly Father, You truly have removed my heart of stone and given me a heart of flesh. Thank You, Lord. Therefore, by Your grace, I will now live as Your New Covenant child, accepting and enjoying Your grace. I love You.

day 2: grace means i'm reconciled!

Focus: Embracing reconciliation

Scripture: As you read Colossians 1:19-22, thank God for your relationship with Him.

Years ago after a misunderstanding with a friend, our relationship became uncomfortably strained. Because of a disagreement, we pulled back from our frequent friend checks. Communication stopped, severing the friendship. I felt devastated, like I'd lost a limb, being separated from my lifelong friend. By God's grace and in His way, we worked it out. We restored our friendship by "agreeing to disagree" instead of arguing about rights and wrongs. We simply put the disagreement issue to rest and the relationship was joyfully restored. That's reconciliation.

Have you ever had a falling out with a good friend? If so, how did you feel about it?

Has your relationship been restored? What are your thoughts about this friendship?

From personal experience I can vouch for the joy that comes with a reconciled relationship. When acceptance and restoration take the place of separation and alienation, there's cause for dancing.

Adam and Eve's disobedience caused a falling out between God and man. God took the initiative to restore the fellowship by sending His Son into the world. Through His shed blood on the cross, Christ reconciled man with God. Because of Christ's love, we are presented blameless before the Father and are now free to enjoy intimacy with Him.

overstating the fact of grace

At the risk of you feeling like I'm hammering this into your brain, I'm going to spend a little more time here. Honestly, I've spent so much of my life living as a "schizophrenic Christian" that I need to review these grace truths daily. As stated in day 1, I've realized that my spiritual framework has been a curious combination of Old Covenant law and New Covenant grace. I know intellectually (and theologically) that I am totally accepted and loved by God, but it seems I can't quite let go of this works mentality, hoping to gain His approval.

Can you relate? ○ yes ○ no

God is gradually doing a work in my life, however, and opening my spiritual eyes. What an exciting and freeing experience, as little by little I grasp these life-changing truths. I'm loving this journey.

How about you? Regarding this grace mystery, are you being freed little by little?
○ yes ○ no ○ not yet, but longing to

What particularly is God speaking to you regarding grace?

There are two critical reasons for you to move into grace-living.

1. **Grace cost Jesus His very life.** By accepting what He so lovingly has given you, you honor Him.
2. **When you understand what grace means** to you personally, you are able and willing to offer it to others. Certainly, there are plenty of people in your life who need grace.

appropriate christian living

By appropriate, I mean suitable and honoring to God. Regarding grace and law, only a life characterized by grace qualifies as living that honors God.

Regarding grace and legalism, circle the word (or phrase) in each statement that most typically describes your behavior and thinking.
Truster of God OR worker to earn His approval?
Burden-bearer OR burden-giver to Jesus?

Do you feel mostly judged or mostly accepted?

Do you feel mostly joy or frustration in your relationship with God?
Is the Christian life hard for you, or is it light and easy?

Are you harassed by a shadow of guilt or enjoying guilt-free living?

If you circled grace responses (you know what they are by now) then you are experiencing Christian living as God designed it for you. If you're not there yet, be encouraged. Take it from me, sometimes it just takes a while. Perhaps you have spent an entire lifetime hunkered down in the law. Give yourself a little grace to make it through, one step at a time. Just keep moving and you'll get there; that's His promise. As Psalm 84:11 says, "For the Lord God is a Sun and Shield; the Lord bestows present grace and favor and future glory! No good thing will He withhold from those who walk uprightly" (AMP).

cloud of guilt

A rather strange sensation pointed me toward the refreshing waters of grace. I had long sensed a wafting layer of guilt like a foreboding fog draped over my spirit. It perplexed me because I could never identify why it was there. As I deeply explored this place of grace in preparation for this study, I believe the Holy Spirit drew back the drapes to allow me to acknowledge and address this thin veil of guilt that had floated unhindered around my consciousness for as long as I could remember. As God opened my spiritual eyes, I became aware of this guilt leech attached to my soul. I knew that it was sucking out morsels of joy and peace, even before I got out of bed each morning.

Remember. This was only a dusting. As I began to embrace His grace, everything in me screamed to rid myself of this intruder. As I tried to identify its origin, "lack of approval" accompanied the air of guilt.

I quickly realized that many psychologists would have a heyday with my psyche at the moment. Indeed, there are times to get professional help in dealing with mental and emotional anguish. But I knew in my heart this was not one of those situations; it was just the New Covenant gal trapped in the Old Covenant shell.

You see, according to God's grace, every touch of sin, shame, and guilt has been removed. We don't need, nor does He desire us, to live with even the smallest diabolic whisper of foreign material to our freed-up soul. Galatians 5:1 reminds us that "Christ has liberated us to be free. Stand firm then and don't submit again to a yoke of slavery."

Final freedom came to me as I recognized the source of the melancholy (Satan's deception and trickery) and claimed the liberty that Christ had already bought.

Here's the beauty of it all; the joy of the freedom far exceeds the air of heaviness that had attached itself to my mind and emotions each morning.

Is a cloud of negativity drooping over your spirit? How about a guilt or disappointment leech attached to your soul, sucking out morsels of joy and peace? You can be assured if you and the Lord have dealt with this matter, it's over. Whatever the dusting of guilt, whether a little or a lot, it doesn't belong there. You can determine right now to cast off any intruder attached to your soul. Just do the following:

1. **Recognize its presence:** Understand it contradicts the grace of God.
2. **Realize that Christ's sacrifice on the cross has freed you:** You have the authority to rebuke the Enemy in this matter, "I order you, intruder to my soul, to leave me alone. You have no authority here!"
3. **Rejoice! Be encouraged:** Your freedom is won, no doubt. You may feel this freedom immediately or gradually. Just keep knowing He's taken care of it.

First John 1:9 tells us that "If we confess our sins, He is faithful and righteous to forgive us our sins and to cleanse us from all unrighteousness." Claim your freedom, girlfriend. Claim it as you sing.

> *Marvelous grace of our loving Lord,*
> *Grace that exceeds our sin and our guilt,*
> *Yonder on Calvary's mount out-poured,*
> *There where the blood of the Lamb was spilt.*
> *Grace, grace, God's grace,*
> *Grace that will pardon and cleanse within;*
> *Grace, grace, God's grace,*
> *Grace that is greater than all our sin."*

Worship with this week's hymn, and scribble your thoughts.

Dear Lord, how can I ever thank You enough for grace? The more I understand about the grace You poured over me when You shed Your blood at Calvary, the more I love You. Thank You for Your grace that pardons and cleanses and truly is greater than all my sin.

Focus: Entering His rest

Scripture: Ask your Heavenly Father to give your mind and emotions rest as you read Matthew 11:25-30.

done with the law

The Lord allowed me a personal experience to illustrate moving from a legalistic mind-set to a grace mind-set. On the evening before I turned my focus to grace for this portion of our journey, I packed up my notes and study materials on the Old Covenant and the Old Testament sacrificial system. It had been one of those glorious days of experiencing God's closeness in study and writing.

Truthfully, I've noticed an unusual abundance of freshness, joy, and energy throughout the preparation of this material—a blessing I've thanked Him for over and over. Personally, I believe it's because I've deliberately turned my attention to His cross, His blood, and His grace. There's nothing more energizing and refreshing than embracing His truth. Freedom and joy abound at every turn. Jesus said it Himself: "You will know the truth, and the truth will set you free." (John 8:32). Free from what? Free from anything that weighs down your spirit.

Check statements below that are true for you now:
- ○ **As I become more cross-centered in my thinking, I feel more at ease emotionally.**
- ○ **Learning to apply His blood has ushered in a new spirit of joy.**
- ○ **I'm beginning to feel freer in my spirit, as I embrace grace.**
- ○ **I've noticed more physical energy as I've gone through this study.**
- ○ **I've noticed more mental clarity to read and understand the Scriptures.**
- ○ **I've had more patience with my family.**
- ○ **My emotions are gradually becoming untangled.**
- ○ **Other** _____

After the "Old Testament pack-up" that night, an unusual fatigue settled over my body and spirit. All of a sudden my body, mind, and emotions just hit a wall. I remember being somewhat perplexed by this rush of heaviness as I went to bed and closed my eyes. Somewhere in the wee hours of the morning, my eyes popped open and my spirit shouted, "I'm done with the law; it's time for grace!" In my semiconscious state, I became aware of an extraordinary peace, joy, and relaxation cascading over me and inside of me as I drifted back to sleep. That's the glorious difference between the heavy burden of the law and the rest and freedom of grace.

moving right along with grace

That's a beautiful illustration, right? Let me take a moment to encourage your heart. You may be thinking, *I wish God would do something like that for me.* I'm figuring that because I used to have thoughts like that all the time. That's the legalistic mind-set kicking in and saying, *If I were good enough, holy enough, or close enough to God, then I'd merit some special divine experiences too.*

Well, you just need to take a second look at the words of Jesus in Matthew 11:25. "I praise You, Father, Lord of heaven and earth, because You have hidden these things from the wise and learned and revealed them to infants."

That's you and me, Girlfriend. It's certainly me, anyway. I don't feel like there's anything wise and learned about me, and I'm totally turning cartwheels over it. I know that the nobody I once thought I was is the somebody Jesus is crazy about.

And I think He loves that I get really caught up in loving Him.

Write three qualities about yourself that God loves. Come on, you can do it! You're not bragging on yourself; you're bragging on God. He gave them to you.

1.

2.

3.

Now. You need to remember this: the Enemy of God who's also the Enemy of God's children is crouched just like a sentinel at your mind's door. He's waiting to gain entry and pounce at any and every opportunity to flip the legalistic switch and put you right back into Old Covenant thinking. He wants to make you think that you're not good enough to hear from God. He wants you to think there's nothing about you that merits any special treatment from Him. Don't let him do that to you. Take control with the authority that is yours through the blood of Jesus Christ and rebuke that detestable vermin.

Satan, you're a liar and a thief! God adores me and sees me through the perfection of Jesus. In the name of Jesus Christ I rebuke you and command you to leave me alone. I am saved by the blood of Jesus Christ who died for me and defeated you. You have no authority over any part of me.

don't settle for less!

Experiencing grace is moving about freely in joy and peace. Any time frustration or other contradictions to God's grace spring forth, you are in the position; indeed you have the authority because of the sacrifice of Jesus to oust this fierce enemy of grace. We should never, as God's children, settle for anything less or accept as normal emotions and mind-sets that are spiritually foreign to our position in Christ.

Remember the cloud of guilt? Accepting it was exactly what I had done for as long as I remember. Most of the time, I didn't pay it any attention because I'd grown accustomed to it hanging around. Not being able to determine its origin made the whole effort of banishing it too involved. So, I let it drape over me like a smothering mist, placing layers of confusion and separation between me and my source of joy—Jesus.

I am so thankful God brought the harassment of the intruder to light. Anything that even slightly undermines your relationship with Jesus Christ can and must be dealt with if you want to pull out all the stops in your relationship with Him.

Have you ever settled for something spiritually foreign to your position in Christ?
○ yes ○ no ○ not sure

At this time in your life, are you accepting as normal something that is spiritually foreign to your position in Christ? ○ yes ○ no

Explain your answer below.

It's time for me to start living happily ever after in God's heart of grace.

Read the above sentence aloud and rewrite it below. Take a few moments to talk it over with the Lord. (You may want to write it on a slip of paper to carry around with you today.)

yoked to legalism or yoked to grace

A yoke is a device that joins together. Jesus invites you to "yoke up" with Him, allowing Him to carry you through your daily circumstances. If you read the passages surrounding our Scripture focal point today, you'll see there was a growing opposition to the ministry of Jesus, particularly among the dogmatic law-keeper Pharisees. As Jesus invites those who are burdened to come to Him, the context of this passage suggests that He is referring to the heavy, self-righteous, legalistic, law-keeping lifestyle of these Pharisees.

When you're yoked with Jesus instead of with the law, the weight's on Him. That makes your part easy. He carries the burden. That makes your load light.

Being an acquaintance of suffering during the past couple of years, my spirit has been comforted time and again as I've basked in the warmth of Jesus' words. His words also soothe my soul when I tip the scales of legalism, getting caught in that "works mentality." Read the passage from The Message paraphrase that follows.

"Are you tired? Worn out? Burned out on religion? Come to me. Get away with me and you'll recover your life. I'll show you how to take a real rest. Walk with me and work with me—watch how I do it. Learn the unforced rhythms of grace. I won't lay anything heavy or ill-fitting on you. Keep company with me and you'll learn to live freely and lightly" (Matt. 11:28-30).

Do you need to get away with Jesus to recover your life? ○ yes ○ no

Worship with this week's hymn, and scribble your thoughts.

Heavenly Father, my heart is longing to be freed of every encumbrance afflicting my soul. I know that even if it's something little that separates us, it's robbing me of the joy of our relationship. It's also displeasing to You for me to accept as normal something that's not. Reveal Your perfect freedom to me and show me how to enjoy You. I love You.

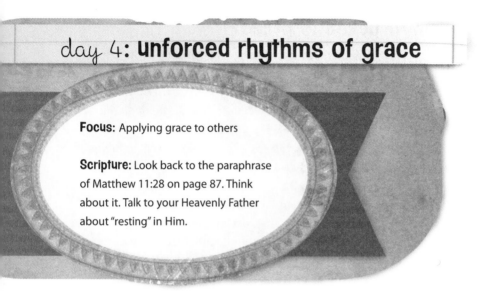

day 4: **unforced rhythms of grace**

Focus: Applying grace to others

Scripture: Look back to the paraphrase of Matthew 11:28 on page 87. Think about it. Talk to your Heavenly Father about "resting" in Him.

Copy Matthew 11:28 on a notecard or slip of paper and carry it with you as a reminder.

the law, ramped up!

If nothing else, the Pharisees were masters of law complication and manipulation. For example, God simply said, "Remember the Sabbath day by keeping it holy" (Ex. 20:8, NIV). Members of this Jewish sect of strict law-keepers were so afraid of earning God's wrath that they took that commandment and came up with over 600 regulations regarding Sabbath keeping. While we may respect their intentions, we would probably agree that many of these laws were ridiculously strict. For instance, one Sabbath law forbade a woman to pick up a needle that she dropped on the floor. The reason? If she picked it up, it might accidentally scratch the dirt floor which would be too much like plowing a field.

Such legalities have a problem. While they may appear to be about honoring God, they produce hollow obedience based on outside actions without any connection to the heart. In fact, such strictness actually creates distance from God rather than intimacy with Him.

Does a "strict law" come to mind that you were forced to obey without understanding what it had to do with honoring God? ○ **yes** ○ **no**

Word of caution: Our purpose is not law-bashing but understanding grace. Make sure you don't get sidetracked.

In defense of holy fierceness, there's something in our nature that is so afraid of not pleasing God that we become overly zealous and often rigid in trying not to offend Him.

glorious freedom

Living under the law makes it difficult for us to accept the freedom of being His child. It's easier for us to think in terms of being a loyal subject to a king. The truth is loyal subjects are not intimate with the king. Their lives are lived proving their loyalty with their actions. On the other hand, the child of the king is free to run about the castle, enjoying the relationship.

In your relationship with the Lord, have you behaved mostly like a subject to the King or like a child of the King? ○ **subject**   ○ **child**

As His child, what freedoms do you long to experience?

Freedom has everything to do with the "unforced rhythms of grace." I love that phrase. There's such a beautiful rhythm to the love of our Lord, sometimes predictable, sometimes not. Grace makes it that way. Grace allows for individuality, differing opinions, expression of a variety of gifts, and seeing things through different eyes. Grace is running about the Kingdom enjoying the King and the many differences in all of His children.

This unforced rhythm of grace also has to do with the many different ways that God's children experience their individual relationships with Him. While I might enjoy exploring the rooms on the east end, my siblings may like roaming around other areas, doing different things.

God's castle is a holy conglomerate of divine delights that are there to be experienced in a variety of ways for all of His children. Grace allows for those differences and simply helps us relish the great assortment of characteristics in God's family. These differences cover styles of worship services and music, as well as individual ways we approach God. Actually, grace covers the way I live my life. I may be different from you in lots of ways and still be right-on with God—imagine that!

We can learn to live in an ongoing unforced rhythm of grace by seeing ourselves and others through the eyes of our Heavenly Father. When I don't busy and bother myself with what's between another person and God, then I have a lot of time leftover for freedom.

Have you ever struggled with viewing your brothers and sisters in God's family with grace as defined above? ○ **yes**   ○ **no**

Explain your answer.

One of the most freeing truths of grace is that it has more to do with the Giver than the recipient. Being an extension of God's grace, I don't concern myself with the response of the recipient; that's between her and God. I just love as God loves and leave the recipient to Him.

In addition, I don't get bogged down with my perception of how others should please God. My part is to please Him personally and allow His other children to please Him as they choose. Again, it's between them and their Heavenly Father.

Is God speaking to your heart right now about the way you view others? If so, explain.

spreading the grace

I'm beginning to experience God's grace personally on a whole new level. I'm learning to take Jesus at His word. As I keep company with Him in the context of all we've explored during these glorious weeks, I'm truly moving closer to that place of living freely and lightly. It's very gradual, but it surely is real.

As you fill your mind with grace awareness, your Heavenly Father will open your understanding of how to apply grace to particular circumstances. He'll give you practice opportunities so that you can become a grace giver and a grace multiplier. And when He presents each situation, you know beyond a shadow of a doubt that it's from Him.

Has God given you an opportunity to practice grace this week? ○ yes   ○ not yet

If yes, explain. If no, expect it soon.

Here's mine: Even though I have the most thoughtful and caring husband, I sometimes make unnecessary requests of him. Can you relate? That happened on morning at breakfast recently. When he hesitated to respond to my request, my feathers were seriously ruffled.

G-R-A-C-E! No, at that moment I didn't ask for it. In fact, grace was the furthest thing from my mind. Ahh, but God. You see He knows when you really want to learn His ways. He hears your cries when you pour out your heart of love to Him, asking Him to make you more like Himself. So He does what any loving parent does; He rushes to your side to give you what you don't even know you need. That's grace.

In the split second before I spewed out words I'd regret, it seemed that the Holy Spirit tapped me on the shoulder and said, "It's OK. Let it go. Practice some grace-giving." In that same second, every bit of angst disappeared and I was washed with total love. In moments, I moved from jaw-clenched, tight-fisted to relaxed, easy living. I'll be quick to tell you that it doesn't always happen immediately as it did that day. But I'm delighted to report that my grace-ometer is more finely tuned than ever. I'm gradually transforming from a not-caring-to-extend-grace person to one who joyfully dishes it out. And here's the sweet reality: I'm pleased, God's pleased, and all the beneficiaries are pleased.

Check the statements below that are true for you.
○ I'm gradually understanding how to give grace to others.
○ I'm gradually becoming aware of God's grace toward me.
○ I'm gradually moving closer to living freely and lightly.
○ There's a new wonder in my heart about the reality of grace.
○ I'm experiencing more joy as I spread more grace.

Worship with this week's hymn, and scribble your thoughts.

Dear Lord, I love the way You are opening my heart and mind to new revelations. The more I learn of You and Your Ways, the more I love You. Again, thank You for the grace You've poured over my life. Teach me to accept all You've given me and to freely give it to others.

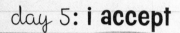

day 5: i accept

Focus: Thankfully receiving God's grace each day

Scripture: Rejoice as you read Romans 5:1-11, thanking God for His indescribable gift.

Marvelous, infinite, matchless grace,
Freely bestowed on all who believe;
All who are longing to see His face,
Will you this moment His grace receive?

Oh, how I long to gaze into my Savior's face and thank Him, thank Him, thank Him for His lavish outpouring of grace on this little frazzled frenetic female. My eyes fill with tears as I think about that moment and as I imagine how it might be. The closest I can get to what it might be like is thinking back to the moment right after my babies were born. As I gazed into those pure and trusting eyes I thought, *This is why I was created.* As I stand before Jesus, surely every smidgen of my being will shout, "For this very moment Lord, this surely is why I was created!"

pause

Close your eyes and ponder the moment you'll come face-to-face with Jesus. Worship Him. Thank Him. Enjoy some time alone with your Savior. Close your study and come back to it later if you wish. Savor these moments. Sometime today or tomorrow, share a portion of your experience in the space below.

One of the marks of spiritual progress is being able to apply life-changing biblical truths to daily circumstances. So far we've explored what the reality of the cross and the benefits of His sacrifice have to do with 21st-century living. This week, we've pressed in a little closer to God's heart by exploring His mysterious grace.

Here's a modern-day picture that comes to mind: You've stopped counting how many times you've told your son to clean his room. The next measure is to post a condemned sign and oust him from the family. Being in sergeant mode one particular morning, you storm into his room (mistake!). Your blood pressure spikes and your eyes shoot fire as you step over one heap of rubble and land in the next. Squaring off with your boy, your eyes lock onto his panic-stricken face.

Now. As the scene unfolds, just suppose without announcement or intimation, love washes over you and takes over. Your bastions of authority melt and your anger vanishes. Right in the middle of this landfill, all you feel is love for your boy. He may deserve the wrath of Mom, but all you want to do is love him.

Underline words and phrases describing the son in the described situation. Circle those describing the mom.

gracious	deserving to be punished
slack	one in authority
negligent	angry at the mess
patient	frightened of judgment
kind	disobedient
forgiving	executor of judgment
disrespectful	full of love
guilty	can't seem to do it right
has final say	extends love instead of what's deserved

The emphasis in this example is not on what's deserved, what needs to be cleaned, or what wrong needs to be righted. The emphasis is on pure love. That's the very essence of mercy and grace.

mercy \ *noun* : not getting what you deserve

grace \ *noun* : getting what you don't deserve

Mercy and grace are in partnership. As Mom enters the quagmire of filth that should be cleaned, instead of dishing out the judgment her son deserves, she is obsessed with loving him.

Is there an experience that comes to mind where you either received mercy and grace or extended mercy and grace? If so, briefly describe.

Take a look at those words you circled and underlined. This time, think about you and God.

As you reflect, write three sentences about God then write three sentences about you.

God
1.
2.
3.

Me
1.
2.
3.

the spiritual truth

1. I've made a horrible mess of things.
2. God sees the mess I'm in and hates it for me.
3. I deserve God's wrath, but I don't get what I deserve (mercy).
4. He sees me, His child (one saved by His blood), and is obsessed with love (grace).

Dear child of God, you may have committed the most abominable sin imaginable, a sin that is so hideous and inexcusable that you truly believe you are outside of God's forgiveness. The only way to experience freedom from shame and guilt is to take God at His word and accept the mercy and grace He purchased for you with His blood shed at Calvary. The Enemy delights when you doubt God. He loves getting back at God through His children. He's behind your reticence to receive the gift of God's grace.

Go ahead and cement this truth deeply inside your heart and mind: Every drop of Christ's shed blood is for you. There is no sin that is not covered by His Sacrifice.

Do you sometimes have difficulty accepting the fact that you really have been forgiven?
○ yes ○ no

First John 1:9 gives simple and clear instructions on receiving what God has secured for you: "If we confess our sins to God, he can always be trusted to forgive us and take our sins away" (CEV).

If you have doubt in your mind about your forgiveness of sins, then let's settle this matter right here and now. Also, it may help you to know that many struggle with accepting forgiveness from God. You are not alone. It just seems too easy and too good to be true.

It is. That's God's grace.

Place a check by each statement describing your Covenant with God.
○ **I have repented of and confessed my sins to God.**
○ **I accept the fact that Jesus died on the cross to save me from God's punishment for these sins.**
○ **I have invited Jesus Christ into my heart as my personal Lord and Savior.**

Your status of salvation is not about feelings. It's about faith. Be assured of this: If you have genuinely sought God's heart in repentance and confession of your sins, then you can trust the fact that He has forgiven you. If you've sincerely invited Him into your heart and life as your personal Lord and Savior, you can know He's there. You must merely accept the fact that you have been forgiven, whether you *feel* forgiven or not. The feelings of doubt that surface from time to time are not in alignment with God's Word, which states that you have been forgiven of all past, present, and future sins.

It doesn't make sense that Mom would stand in the middle of that pigsty of filth and spew forth love instead of vengeance. But more amazing than that is the fact that our Savior Jesus left the glory of heaven to dwell in the hovel of humanity. Instead of dishing out the judgment we deserved, He conquered this sin-infested world with mercy and grace. As we close this week's study, allow His grace truths to steep in your heart.

Worship with this week's hymn, and scribble your thoughts.

Dear Heavenly Father, You understand more than I do the Enemy's goal to make me doubt Your grace. Energize me with Your truth today. Free my spirit and my mind to believe. Open my eyes to new revelations about Your love and grace. I trust You and I love You so much.

At the Cross

Alas, and did my Savior bleed,

And did my Sovereign die?

Would He devote that sacred head

For such a worm as I?

But drops of grief can never repay

The debt of love I owe;

Here, Lord, I give myself away,

'Tis all that I can do!

At the cross,

at the cross where I first saw the light,

And the burden of my heart rolled away,

It was there by faith I received my sight,

And now I am happy all the day!

—Isaac Watts, 1707
Chorus, Ralph E. Hudson, 1885

5

my
eyesight
restored
at the
cross

day 1: remember the light

Focus: Focusing on the cross

Scripture: As you read 2 Corinthians 4:1-6, thank your Heavenly Father for revealing His light.

Sing this glorious melody and let it warm your heart.

At the cross, at the cross where I first saw the light,
And the burden of my heart rolled away,
It was there by faith I received my sight,
And now I am happy all the day!

creatures of habit

Yes, we are. Just drop by your favorite fast-food restaurant or coffee shop at the same time every day for a week and notice who's there, besides you. And if you look closer, you'll probably notice people behaving in the same way each day. We seem to find comfort in establishing daily rituals. These habits bring us security and establish our priorities. Whether it's nestling in our favorite spot to browse the Internet or reading a special book before going to bed, we love our daily habits.

Habits cover all sorts of behaviors and revolve around things like food, exercise, thought patterns, routines having to do with different times of day, and so forth.

Circle areas below that are connected with some of your personal habits.

foods	morning routines	nightly routines
house cleaning	entertainment	devotion time
family activities	clothing	weekend routines
weekday routines	phone calls	exercise
computer time	driving	other _____

Explain how and why one of your habits began.

developing godly habits

We make time for what's important. We create habits and routines around things and people we value. Establishing a new habit doesn't always come easily, but we persevere and make it so because we want to incorporate it into our daily lives. It's a gloriously divine training process when it's a godly habit we're working on.

When I initiated my personal habit of getting up early to spend time with God, I was a busy young mother with a full-time teaching job. In order to have those moments with the Lord I so desperately wanted, I had to get up at 4:30 a.m. I remember falling asleep morning after morning. It was tough, but I became a stubborn woman on a mission to get alone with God. By His grace, I persevered until a "new norm for Cindi" was birthed. That's been quite a few years ago, but that habit remains fixed as a priority in my life.

Do you have a godly habit that is rooted in your life? If so, list it below.

Was it tough at first establishing this new pattern? Why or why not?

What suggestion would you give a girlfriend wanting to begin the same discipline?

my "remember the cross" mission

With my new revelations about Christ's sacrificial love and the benefits belonging to me as His child, I've become eager and joyful in establishing new habits of focusing on the cross. Every day, I think about the truths I've learned surrounding His blood and His grace. For me, it's exhilarating to review and meditate on those Old Testament Scripture passages that point to His sacrifice, now that I more deeply understand them. Yes siree, I'm going back to my spiritual roots and grabbing hold of a newly recognized joy that's causing me to dance and sing and twirl around in His love. Psalm 68:3 says, "When the righteous see God in action they'll laugh, they'll sing, they'll laugh and sing for joy" (Message).

Here are simple ways I keep my cross passion fresh and exciting every day.

I sing cross songs. Sometimes I sing these during my early morning worship time. Quite often, I sing them while driving. There are many beautiful old and newer contemporary songs about the cross. The old hymns we've set aside for this study are especially meaningful to me because they mark my deeper understanding and increased love for my Savior because of His sacrifice at Calvary.

Name a particular cross song that has special meaning for you.

Why is it special? When do you sing it?

I embrace Scriptures about the cross. By embrace I mean take and receive gladly what God's Word says about His death and resurrection. For example, Ephesians 2:1-10 causes me to think about and celebrate my new life in Christ as opposed to my dead carnality before His resurrection. In my devotion each day, I include a passage about His blood, grace, or sacrifice. I pause during the day and deliberately think about these things. His Word has become more personal and meaningful as I go through my day.

What Scripture passage has become personal and meaningful since you began this study? Why is it significant to you?

I thank Him. My heart has undergone such regeneration as I've become acquainted with and embraced the cross. More often than not, I can't sing cross songs or study cross Scriptures without exploding in thankfulness. But even on those days when I don't feel the ecstasy, I speak words of thankfulness for His death and resurrection. A thankful heart keeps the message of the cross alive in my heart and mind.

Feel free to share about a recent special time of thankfulness.

I keep the cross before me visually. If you don't share my personality style, this may come across as rather cheesy, so remember to extend some grace. With a marker, I place a small cross on my big toe. You see, my heart "has it" but my mind and will need some spiritual boot camp training. As I step through my day, this visual reminder trains me to move forward keeping the sacrifice of Jesus fresh on my mind.

Is there a practical way you have trained your mind to focus on the cross of Christ? (If you haven't yet done this, you may share later.)

I memorize Scripture. Whatever the need, there's a Scripture to match. For instance, when I struggle with a guilt issue, I memorize a Scripture about the forgiveness of sin. Memorizing verses about His grace helps me experience His freedom in my thought life. Tucking verses in my heart and mind about His blood keeps me engaged with His power. Scripture memory comes so much easier when you understand the passage and make its message personal to you. Take a look at the verses included in "The Scripture Garden" at the end of this study. They are relevant to our content and will jump-start your Scripture memory journey.

Think of a Scripture you want to memorize. What is it?

Why is it special to you?

I deliberately think about the cross when I wake up and before going to sleep. I love tucking my day between thoughts of the cross. Because of His sacrifice, each day holds fresh meaning. Accepting His grace has ushered me into new areas of freedom I never thought possible. Appropriating His power is now something I do regularly instead of occasionally. Realizing the impact the cross has on my life, I want to honor the Lord with thankfulness as soon as my eyes pop open and at day's end as I drift off to sleep. Yes, holy bookends supporting my day.

As we close today's study, what's the Father revealing to you?

Worship with this week's hymn, and scribble your thoughts.

Dear Heavenly Father, Your cross is deeply impacting my life. Help me, by Your grace, become more cross focused and cross thankful. As I develop godly habits that will remind me of Your love, please keep me bolstered and encouraged through Your Holy Spirit. I long to experience all of You, Lord. Thank You for loving me and giving me Yourself.

day 2: **safe and secure**

Focus: Understanding your security
in Jesus

Scripture: Ask God to reveal new truths
as you read Genesis 7:1-16.

lost

Nothing shoots fear up my spine like the sudden realization that I'm lost. Unsettling childhood memories flood my mind of being swept up in a crowd and separated from my parents. That same noxious fear still jolts my nerves when I get lost from my husband or children. Other times, it's when I'm traveling alone and suddenly realize I'm in uncharted territory that waves of panic shatter my peace.

Nothing in me likes feeling lost, so I'm greatly relieved when I inevitably find my husband or kids around the corner and the road that disappeared from the map shows up again. I delightfully confess that moments of angst that grip my heart during my feeling-lost moments eventually and always lead me to thankfulness that I'm safe and secure.

Have you felt similar panic and insecurity over being lost? If so, describe your experience.

forever saved

Through the years of our ministry, I've run across those who struggle with the assurance of staying saved. They've professed faith in the Son of God and yet are panicked at the thought of losing their salvation. They quickly affirm that they at one time moved from being lost to being saved but have struggled on and off since that moment with thoughts of falling out of that saved position. My heart ached as they described their mental battles and poured out longings to know for certain that there was no way they could lose their salvation or their position in Jesus Christ. For some, the struggle was directly tied to entering into willful sin after they'd accepted Christ as Savior. For others, it had more to do with daily choices that would cause them to fall out of favor with God.

Have you ever struggled with feelings of losing your salvation or known others who have struggled with feelings of losing their salvation? ○ yes ○ no

Let's look at God's Word, our authority, so you can rejoice in the assurance that you and your salvation are indeed safe and secure in Jesus Christ.

Truth.

Anyone who willingly and humbly repents of sin, embracing the Truth of the cross—trusting Jesus as Lord and Savior—is saved. "God loved the world in this way: He gave His One and Only Son, so that everyone who believes in Him will not perish but have eternal life" (John 3:16). At the moment you believe, you become God's child, and He, your Heavenly Father. This is only made possible through the shed blood of Jesus on the cross. You cannot get out of a "blood relation." The prodigal son did not cease to be his father's child when he deliberately entered into rebellion (see Luke 15:11-32). God's child cannot get out of God's family.

Place a _T_ for true or _F_ for false beside each statement.
___ When I enter into a relationship with Jesus, my salvation can never be taken away from me.
___ When I deliberately or inadvertently rebel, I am no longer part of God's family.

Truth.

If you have genuinely invited Jesus Christ into your heart as your personal Lord and Savior, you cannot lose your salvation. Jesus Himself said, "I give them eternal life, and they will never perish—ever! No one will snatch them out of My hand" (John 10:28). You, by your sin, cannot snatch yourself out of the saving hand of Jesus Christ. To suggest so casts doubt on the secure grasp of our Savior.

Place a _T_ for true or _F_ for false beside each statement.
___ Jesus said, "I give them eternal life. No one can snatch them out of My hand."
___ No sin or person can pry open the secure grasp of Jesus Christ on my life.

Truth.

Jesus' sacrifice was a one-time occurrence that covered every sin. "He entered the most holy place once for all, not by the blood of goats and calves, but by His own blood, having obtained eternal redemption" (Heb. 9:12). The idea of going from a saved position to an unsaved one is simply not scriptural. If you could lose your salvation, then it would be lost forever because Jesus only died once. It is impossible to be re-redeemed. Nowhere in the Bible does anyone get saved a second time.

Place a *T* for true or *F* for false beside each statement.
___ There are some sins His sacrifice does not cover.
___ Jesus died once which means that one sacrifice covers every sin.

Truth.

When we enter into salvation, God places His deposit of the Holy Spirit within us. "When you heard the message of truth, the gospel of your salvation, and when you believed in Him, you were also sealed with the promised Holy Spirit. He is the down payment of our inheritance, for the redemption of the possession, to the praise of His glory" (Eph. 1:13-14). God's deposit in us is His Holy Spirit, God Himself. His deposit secures our salvation. God cannot lose Himself.

How can God's deposit, His Holy Spirit, help you during times of doubting?

Truth.

Not accepting eternal security is refuting God's grace. "You are saved by grace through faith, and this is not from yourselves; it is God's gift" (Eph. 2:8). To suggest that children of God can do something to fall out of salvation is in direct opposition to God's grace. Critics of the "once saved, always saved doctrine" claim that it gives Christians the license to sin, presuming that those who have their eternal security guaranteed will then continue in earthly sin because they can get away with it.

From your walk with Jesus Christ and your knowledge of His sacrifice, what assurance can you offer those who claim His grace is a license to sin?

noah's ark, portrait of security

"A male and female of each kind entered, just as God had commanded Noah. Then the LORD closed the door behind them" (Gen. 7:16, NLT). Noah moved in obedience in the building of the ark. He moved in obedience in loading up the ark with the animals and his family. Noah obeyed as God directed. Then God shut the door. What great truth is found in this passage, the very picture of who we are in Christ.

one door

One door was God's design for the ark. By entering through it, Noah and his family were guaranteed safety. Then God closed the door. Jesus Christ is the "one door" in God's blueprint for salvation. When you enter in through that door, God shuts you in. God Himself guarantees your safety and security based on the life of His Son. "I am the door. If anyone enters by Me, he will be saved" (John 10:9).

one salvation

Once Noah and his family were safely inside the ark, the floodgates of the sky were opened. I'm sure that boat rocked and rolled causing all inside to often lose their footing, crash into walls, and topple over each other. Most likely, they felt insecure and unstable, but the reality was they were totally safe in the grasp of God. By entering through the door He provided, they chose life on the inside, rejecting certain death that was the fate of all left on the outside of God's place of safety.

one door leading to one salvation

If you have genuinely invited Him into your life as your Lord and Savior, it is a matter of honor, faith, and trust that you never doubt your salvation. Doubting you've been saved is casually dismissing His death and resurrection. It's saying, "Lord, I know You said You died once for me and with Your sacrifice, I'm saved for all eternity, but …"

At any moment you move away from the truth of eternal security, you're adding your stuff to God's grace. Your message to God is, "I know Your grace has saved me, but let me add a little of *my* works to the mix." That's not scriptural, and it's an affront to Holy God.

My friend, as we close today's study, will you thank your Father and Savior for His one-time sacrifice? Write your prayer of thankfulness. Conclude today's study time by worshiping to the lyrics of "At The Cross."

day 3: dressed in righteousness

Focus: Enjoying your holy clothing

Scripture: Slowly read Isaiah 61:1-3,10-11.
Imagine standing in the Lord's presence
as He clothes you in His righteousness.

during the night

Once again, tears fill my eyes and wonder explodes in my heart as I think about a
special dream I had years ago. It seems I've experienced the tenderness of the Lord
on many occasions during the middle of the night. These hours seem to position
me to hear from Him. The cacophony of the day often drowns out His voice, but
at night my soul is finally at rest. It's during these moments that I seem to hear my
Lord speak more clearly than ever.

Have you had a special moment with God during the night? If so, share your experience.

wearing His robe

Here's the dream that I still can't get out of my mind and hope I never will. I was
a little girl standing in front of a big closet filled with the most beautiful little girl
dresses I'd ever seen. They were dazzling and elegant, and I imagined how pretty I
might look in them. In the middle of that little girl reverie, another little girl skipped
to my side and in a taunting tease remarked, "You can look at them, but you can't
put them on." Then, Jesus appeared on the other side of me. Without hesitation
He took off His beautiful robe and smiled saying, "Here, wear this. It's my robe of
righteousness."

Are you wearing His robe of righteousness? If you're a child of His, you have
it on. And it didn't just magically drape over you. Lovingly and sacrificially, the
King Himself permanently placed it on you with the offering of His blood on the

cross. His sacrifice is your robe. "I greatly rejoice in the LORD, I exult in my God; for He has clothed me with the garments of salvation and wrapped me in a robe of righteousness" (Isa. 61:10).

**Have you ever pictured yourself wearing His robe of righteousness? ○ yes ○ no
If so, describe your thoughts.**

gloriously swaddled

A precious visual comes to mind. After the births of each grandchild, I've spent weeks in the homes of my children. Time and again, I've watched these loving parents swaddle their babies as they've placed them in bed at night. They gingerly caressed and turned them, being careful to tuck in every edge of the cloth so that they were completely snuggled safely inside the blanket. Oh how peaceful, secure, and content they appeared to be each time they were swaddled.

pause

Take a swaddle moment right now. Spend some time here, not getting in a hurry. Give yourself the luxury of visualizing being clothed and swaddled in the robe of righteousness by King Jesus Himself. It doesn't matter how you imagine the moment. Maybe you're standing like the little girl in the dream, or maybe you're being swaddled as you fall off to sleep at night. The critical part is that you acknowledge the reality that you are indeed wearing His robe of righteousness and that Jesus has placed it around you. You are gently and securely tucked in through His death and resurrection.

Describe your moment.

How does this vision affect you?

beautiful clothing

Awaking from the dream that night, the image of those beautiful clothes stuck with me. I thought of times when I'd felt like absolute royalty, all because I was dressed up. One glowing memory took me back to the night I wore the red velvet dress my grandmother made for me to wear to my first-ever youth Christmas party. It mattered not that I'd dribbled toothpaste down the front in my excitement to get out the door. Even traipsing through mud puddles on the way to the car didn't phase me one bit. I was a princess, and for the next few hours, absolutely nothing dampened my spirits. I felt ecstatic, confident, and truly regal being all dressed up.

Do you have a special dress-up memory? If so, share some highlights below.

Circle adjectives that describe how you feel today when you are wearing something you consider to be beautiful.

happy	confident	in-control	positive	bold
beautiful	comfortable	encouraged	excited	radiant
elegant	classy	admired	energized	other _____

kick up your heels

It's party time, girls! It's time for all of us to get off our spiritual duffs and celebrate who we are. It's time to enjoy what we're wearing. As Isaiah 52:1-2 says, "Wake up, wake up! Pull on your boots. ... Dress up in your Sunday best. ... Brush off the dust and get to your feet" (Message). This is a call to jolt us out of our spiritual dullness and lethargy so that we can encourage each other with the truth of God.

How frequently are you joyful about being clothed in His righteousness?
(Place an X on the line below.)

---

never   from time to time   often   all the time

God gave me a gift that night. My little girl dream deepened my understanding of His righteousness and what it means to me personally. He showed me a glorious picture of the sanctity of His redeemed. Such a loving God He is to remind me of this glorious truth in a way I could truly get it.

Since that dream years ago, I more often picture myself wearing His robe of righteousness—my royal clothing, according to Scripture. Seeing myself in this way helps me walk in a manner worthy of the attire.

How might awareness of wearing your robe of righteousness impact you in these areas?
emotions:
daily schedules:
interactions with others:
self-esteem:
serving others:
stress level:
other:

Tomorrow we'll take a look at what it actually means to wear that holy clothing. But for the rest of today, remember this: Belonging to the King, you're not just any child running around the castle; you're a princess wearing your King's holy robes. You're decked out in fine linen without spot or wrinkle. It matters not that you've fallen in the mud or dribbled toothpaste down the front of your beautiful clothing. He sees only the beauty of His righteous robe! "She was given fine linen to wear, bright and pure" (Rev. 19:8).

Worship with this week's hymn, and scribble your thoughts.

Oh Father, give me Your eyes to see myself wearing Your beautifully white and spotless robe of righteousness. I do believe I have it on, but I need Your vision and Your power to help me remember I'm wearing it. Thank You so much for clothing me, swaddling me, and tucking me in securely with Your firm touch. I feel so happy and secure being wrapped in Your love. I love You, Your Princess.

Focus: Understanding my responsibility

Scripture: Read Revelation 19:8, Isaiah 52:1; 61:10. Think about what wearing His righteousness means to you personally.

the meaning

As we consider these passages, we're drawn to the picture of the bride of Christ—you. You are His bride and you're all decked out in your garments of salvation, including garland, jewels, and all the holy glitter you can imagine. Yes, you are arrayed in the pure splendor of God's glory. What a true and beautiful picture of the sanctity of the redeemed.

It's important that you spend time getting this picture of you tucked in the forefront of your mind. Maybe you're hearing the world shout, "There's nothing beautiful about you!" But God's Word boasts differently. Just as an earthly bride enjoys all the bridal hoopla surrounding her wedding day, God's divine plan is for you to enjoy—yes, truly enjoy—being His bride.

Our immediate family has experienced three weddings in recent years, and I've thoroughly enjoyed every bit of festivity. I commented to my husband that I'd love to get married again (to him, of course) and have every moment surrounding our wingding filled with extravagant joy and celebration—sans the stress. From preparing the bride (me) to embracing the bridegroom (him) and celebrating the marriage (us), it would be a red-letter day with feasting, dancing, and merrymaking.

Pretend that you, the bride, are making bridal preparations. Forget the stress and focus on the fun of preparing yourself for your groom. Place a check by all you'd enjoy.
- ○ a new color invented just for me to top off a luxurious manicure and pedicure
- ○ a massage that relaxes me before the wedding bells chime
- ○ a facial that wipes away every wrinkle of stress and age
- ○ beautiful clothing giving me an elegant, classy, and desirable charm
- ○ dancing shoes gracefully gliding me all over the dance floor

○ scrumptious party foods with all calories removed
○ beautiful music lifting our celebration to the heavens
○ inexhaustible energy so I could celebrate forever
○ other _____

Now. Transfer your hopes and dreams of an earthly celebration to the reality of your spiritual status. My friend, never should a single day pass without celebration of the fact that you are the bride of Christ, without a spot or wrinkle and bedecked in fine linen, according to Revelation 19. The fine linen, your righteousness, is your clothing of holy splendor. It is truly His doing. In ourselves, we're disgustingly offensive. "We are all as an unclean thing, and all our righteousnesses are as filthy rags" (Isa. 64:6, KJV).

Nothing we can do can possibly earn our salvation. God only can remove guilt and give us new clothing. "I have removed your guilt from you, and I will clothe you with splendid robes" (Zech. 3:4).

However, we do have responsibility in the matter. Our part is to aspire with all of our heart and soul and mind, to walk in a manner befitting the bride of Christ.

Circle areas in which your heart longs to walk in a manner befitting the bride of Christ.

with children	with nonbelievers	in the workplace
at church	with husband	in your community
with parents	in ministry	other _____

trash the dress

If you've never heard of this wedding photography style, let me enlighten you. "Trashing the dress" takes the elegance of the bride and her bridal clothing and places them in an environment out of context with the beauty and splendor that belong to them. The bride in her gown might run into the ocean or lie down in mud, essentially covering the white dress with stains and imperfections. Many times it's done as an additional shoot after the wedding, signifying the dress will be put away or never worn again.

Curious, to be sure; and the spiritual parallel staggers me.

The unbeliever meets the Savior and enters into a relationship with Him being the love of her life. He places His glorious robe of righteousness around her and she becomes His bride for all of eternity. Later, maybe even years later, she—wearing that beautifully pure and righteous robe—fails to remember the holy drama that took place on her behalf. Casually she may dismiss the fact that she is still clothed in righteousness and eventually trashes the dress, spiritually speaking.

How? By failing to thank Him for righteousness, engaging in unholy conduct, having an unforgiving spirit, criticizing self and others, and forgetting to seek Him with whole heart and soul and mind, to name a few.

If you're like many Christians, little by little the stains of the world have clouded your awareness of who you are in Christ. Maybe you have mentally put away your dress of righteousness, forgetting your purity and holiness in the eyes of God.

Often, we even forget we are wearing it in the first place.

Stop. Mentally put that clean white dress back on. Thanks be to God for continually washing away each and every stain. "I wipe away your sins because of who I am. And so, I will forget the wrongs you have done" (Isa. 43:25, CEV).

Oh, what hope. What glory! What true celebration is ours because of what Christ our Bridegroom has done for us.

keeping consistent

I long to wear my holy clothing with integrity. In other words, I want my lifestyle to match my robe. Here are some steps I'm taking.

1. **I'm getting to know Him.** Honestly, this step is the answer to every spiritual hankering I've ever had. I'm not talking about mildly seeking Him, but I now have a craving to learn everything I possibly can about Him, knowing His attributes, His personality, His desires, His mind. The more I discover, the more I long to walk in His righteousness. Our love for each other keeps me faithful.

2. **I'm living with thanksgiving.** The more I get to know Him, the deeper in love I fall with my Savior. And swirling in that knowledge and love is a heart bursting with thanksgiving. I'm remembering to thank Him when I wake up and just before I drop off to sleep. My growing knowledge and deeper love are giving voice to songs and prayers of thankfulness throughout each and every day.

There's nothing revolutionary or innovative about the ideas of getting to know Him and thanking Him. That's the point. It's not difficult or strange or unimaginable. You understand how to get to know someone and how to be thankful. So, you just do it.

Do you desire to flow in your robe of righteousness with integrity?   ○ yes   ○ not sure

Our entire study has been one of returning to the cross, our spiritual birthplace. For weeks now, we've opened our hearts and minds to loving Him, thanking Him, and living daily with His love and grace empowering us. He is delighted by your genuine heart of love for Him. "The LORD your God is living among you. He is a mighty savior. He will take delight in you with gladness. ... He will rejoice over you with joyful songs" (Zeph. 3:17, NLT).

Personally, I'm not concerned with the "trashing the dress" craze, earthly speaking. But spiritually speaking, I've become a determined bride; determined to keep my earthly and spiritual walk consistent with the holy robe I'm wearing.

Write to your Heavenly Father, telling Him of your desire to walk worthily as His bride.

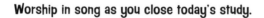

Worship in song as you close today's study.

Thank You Jesus, my Bridegroom, for caressing me in Your robe of righteousness. Continue to draw me deeper into Your love, as I seek You and thank You. I love You.

day 5: my worminess, His worthiness

Focus: Understanding the nature of your relationship with Christ

Scripture: Meditate on God's holiness as you spend some time with Revelation 4:11.

Going back to my Christian roots, I remember barely being able to see over the pews in front of me when I first learned to sing one of the most honored and beloved hymns in all of Christianity, "At The Cross." In our small North Carolina church, we sang it just the way Isaac Watts penned it in 1707, "Would He devote that sacred head for such a worm as I?"

Did you learn the "worm" version of "At The Cross"? ○ yes ○ no

How have you heard this phrase revised?

Yes, it was through *The Broadman Hymnal* (copyright 1940) where I first learned I was a worm. Oh, but a worm so loved by God that He devoted His sacred head to cover all my sins. As years passed and new editions of Baptist hymnals released, "such a worm as I" was replaced with "sinners such as I" or "such a one as I."

Now girls, my streak of rebellion that flares up from time to time keeps me insistent on singing worm when those around me are singing the more palatable versions. I have noticed, however, that I'm not alone. It appears that some others who learned the worm lyrics as children seem to have problems with the upgrade.

While some may see this as merely semantics, I see it as a subtle watering down of the truth of my place before a holy God. Isaiah 43:4 tells us that we are precious and honored in God's sight. "We are unfit to worship you; each of our good deeds is merely a filthy rag. We dry up like leaves; our sins are storm winds sweeping us away" (CEV).

That's worm status right there. When I casually begin to see myself as anything better than a "filthy rag" in relation to God's holiness, I'm not only diluting, I'm polluting the gospel of Jesus Christ. Paul wrote "I am astonished that you are so quickly deserting the one who called you by the grace of Christ and are turning to a different gospel" (Gal. 1:6, NIV).

We live in an era where the gospel of self-esteem runs rampant. Many soar to new heights of importance on the wings of self-worth, thus dismissing all in out sufficiency in Jesus Christ. The disciplines of self-denial, self-sacrifice, and self-abandonment have all but phased out of many teaching materials and messages.

Listen: It's not until we realize that we are worms—dirty on the outside and filled with dirt on the inside—that our hearts are riveted with the truth about grace. Only then, with our status clearly defined, are we positioned to receive all the Lord has for us.

Thoughts?

Lest you think I'm over the top and throwing all the post-worm hymnals under the bus, I assure you my desire is merely to redirect our hearts and minds to who we are before a holy God. As Isaiah 41:14 says, "Do not fear, you worm Jacob, you men of Israel: I will help you—this is the LORD's declaration. Your Redeemer is the Holy One of Israel."

You see, worm status is in direct opposition to what the world promotes: self-glorification, self-worth, self-rights. And all too often, Christians have fallen right in line with this popular self-esteem philosophy. Before you know it, we're right there with the world, touting our rights and shouting our demands, moving in our own flow instead of turning to our Father for help and direction.

It's easy to be pulled into the "all about me" mentality. There's something about that line of reasoning that feels right and self-protecting. However, personally speaking, it doesn't take me long to move from self-attention to nursing my secret hurts and mentally going through my list of what I deserve and don't deserve. Thought by thought, I become distracted from God and preoccupied with Cindi. And, if I keep following that path, that tower eventually crumbles, taking all my rights and demands along with it. Before I know it, all my hurts and self-centered dreams lay scattered in a hopeless pile of junky debris.

Has this ever happened to you? ○ **yes** ○ **no**

If so, explain.

safer and happier

Have you ever fallen totally prostrate? I'm talking face down on the ground in submission and adoration before your Lord. That's worm positioning. When I collapse before Him like that in worship, everything in me wants to go lower.

In that divine moment, lowest becomes highest. When I'm completely surrendered and seeing myself as nothing and Him as everything, He seems to swoop me up and infuse me with His glorious power and joy. My entire being shouts right along with Paul, "My life is worth nothing to me unless I use it for finishing the work assigned me by the Lord Jesus—the work of telling others the Good News about the wonderful grace of God" (Acts 20:24, NLT).

During those awesome moments of worship and awareness of who I am before my holy God, I know without a doubt that He alone is worthy to receive all glory, honor, and praise. I'm so fully aware during that holy instant that the only reason I was created is to bring Him pleasure and glory.

Have you ever had a moment when you were exceptionally aware of God's glory?
○ yes   ○ not yet

How did you feel?

I've discovered the safest place for me to ever live is in total awareness of the glory and strength of my God and not the sufficiency of Cindi. My heart, my mind, and my entire being remain healthy and thriving as long as I remember *who* I am and *where* I came from. It has nothing to do with self-abasement and everything to do with God glorification.

Yes indeed, this gal's created, valued, and loved—birthed in my Father's bosom and tucked inside His heart. As Isaiah 43:4 tells me I am precious and honored in His sight. So recognizing that I'm a worm is not about devaluing self but recognizing and accepting who I really am in the holy scheme of things.

I realize I'm taking great liberty here, but may I just say, "I will most gladly boast all the more about my worminess, so that Christ's power may reside in me" (2 Cor. 12:9, my adaptation with a "worminess").

How has today's study affected you?

embracing His holiness

Today's topic is an appropriate segue to the final week of our journey: holiness.

Next week we will boldly approach His throne, because we can do that, according to Hebrews 4:16. That thought makes me tremble. My goal for the last days of our holy excursion is to bring us gently and boldly into His holy presence. Focusing *all* of me on *all* of Him.

As for now, let's close out our appointed time with our Lord in worship.

You may choose to fall humbly before Him in gratitude and praise. Or maybe you'd like to sing "At The Cross" as you bow your head and heart. Personalizing Revelation 4:11 and praying it back to Him would be beautifully acknowledging who He is and who you are in His presence. Write your prayer or thoughts as you desire below. Take your time. Enjoy His presence.

My Lord and my God, You are worthy to receive all glory and honor and power. You created all things. You created me. I love You.

Holy, Holy, Holy

Holy, holy, holy! Lord God Almighty!

Early in the morning

our song shall rise to Thee;

Holy, holy, holy! merciful and mighty!

God in three Persons, blessed Trinity!

Holy, holy, holy!

all the saints adore Thee,

Casting down their golden crowns

around the glassy sea;

Cherubim and seraphim

falling down before Thee,

Who wert, and art, and

evermore shalt be.

—Reginald Heber, 1826

6

there's something holy going on

a note from cindi

Approaching the final week of our study, I've made many attempts to put words to paper. Each time, holy hesitation locked my fingers. Time and again, this caution from Ecclesiastes halted me and caused me to silence my mind and body, as I humbly knelt before my holy God. "Do not be quick with your mouth, do not be hasty in your heart to utter anything before God. God is in heaven and you are on earth, so let your words be few" (Eccl. 5:2, NIV).

For this reason, I'm breaking all the Bible study rules for our last week together. There are five divisions, but they are not written in a daily format. Journey through them as you feel led.

I'm aware that little by little my life is changing, as He refreshes my soul with His Word. As I am getting to know Him, My understanding is increasing and my longing for Him is deepening. As you are getting to know Him, perhaps you feel the same arrest in your spirit. Even though our journeys are different, we've each traveled through the same sacred content. Together, we've studied how Jesus fulfilled the requirements of the old sacrificial system by becoming our personal sacrificial Lamb. Because of His shed blood on our behalf, we can now enter into the holiest of all, God's presence. We are one of His own; indeed we are one in Him, with our meager bodies becoming the place of His holy dwelling. His mercy, grace, and love are unfathomable, unexplainable, and mysteriously baffling.

At this moment, it seems His glory is overpowering me. It is simply too much for me to take in, let alone to articulate.

I do know He has brought me to a place of hallowed trembling in my heart. I've come to know Him as my dearest and most intimate friend; but not just any friend—He is holy God.

So. Now is the proper time and place for us to acknowledge and respond to His holiness. In keeping with the counsel from Ecclesiastes, we'll close our study in this nontraditional style. You'll not see the usual daily format with questions and blanks for you to fill in. I'll present an overview, leaving you the freedom to proceed as the Holy Spirit leads. Truthfully, you may want to spend days or weeks with one theme. Indeed, each segment may usher in a lifelong change for you, as you enter into a new divine relationship paradigm with the Lord. Invite the Holy Spirit to guide you as you nestle deeply inside God's heart, your home.

Join me. Together we'll run throughout the castle exploring and enjoying His freedom as He delights in bringing us further up and deeper in. With few words and singular devotion, we will approach the holiness of God. He told us we could. As Hebrews 4:16 reminds us, "Let us approach the throne of grace with boldness."

Desperate

beholding His glory

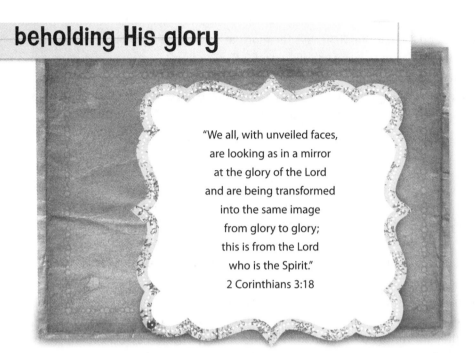

"We all, with unveiled faces,
are looking as in a mirror
at the glory of the Lord
and are being transformed
into the same image
from glory to glory;
this is from the Lord
who is the Spirit."
2 Corinthians 3:18

Do you long for change; a transformation in your soul that will produce persever-ance in the thick of trials, energy in the midst of stress and pressures, strength and stability when your world is rocking, joy when your heart is shredding, and wisdom when your mind is confounded?

Authentic, vibrant change comes from fixing your eyes and planting your heart on Jesus. Continually gazing on who God was, who God is, and who God forever more will be will transform you from one degree of glory to another. I'm talking about actively and continually gazing at Him throughout every day.

The principle is this: What is important enough for you to spend your time and energy on, you will become. You will experience the glory of God, to the degree you gaze at the glory of God. Focusing on the reality of who He is will gradually reveal the reality of His holiness. As you repeatedly contemplate who He is and where He dwells in Scripture, these facts will become more tangible. God will progressively become more real. Heavenly sights, sounds, and holiness will gradually become as familiar to you as your earthly reality.

With your understanding increasing and your heart opening to heavenly truths, you will see Him for who He truly is and desperately long for more intimacy with Him. He will make it so.

Moses beheld Him. So did Ezekiel, Isaiah, Daniel, and John. They didn't understand everything about these visions; neither will you. The finite will never understand the infinite. But that's the glorious mystery of it all. Here's the point: You can choose to become captivated with God.

Today, you can begin to focus on God's glory. You can purpose in your mind and heart to go searching for Him in a way you've never done before. You'll be changed, and you won't be disappointed.

God's promise

Jeremiah 29:13 says, "When you come looking for me, you'll find me. Yes, when you get serious about finding me and want it more than anything else, I'll make sure you won't be disappointed" (Message).

Read aloud Revelation 4:1-11. This will help keep your mind focused.

I began reading this passage aloud several times a day many months ago. I've discovered that I am now viewing God more as who He really is, instead of who I've thought Him to be. Communion with Him is deepening. I'm becoming more aware of Him on His heavenly throne. His presence in the flashes of lightning and rumblings of thunder are becoming more of a reality. My vision of God is becoming more accurate as I focus on who He is in Scripture.

At some point, you'll want to give words to your experience. How is focusing on who He really is changing you? You may record this today, tomorrow, or weeks from now. I know it's difficult to put His glory on paper, but chronicling your journey will help you keep your encounter with God up close and personal. (Visit "The Scripture Garden" for additional passages which focus on God's glory.)

Journal your experience as you feel led.

Dear Heavenly Father, thank You for moving me from one degree of glory to another. Keep my longing for You deep and personal. Keep me at it when I don't feel Your presence or feel like gazing at You. I give You my heart and my intention, thanking You for what You are about to do. I want to see Your glory. Amen.

the fragrance of sacrifice

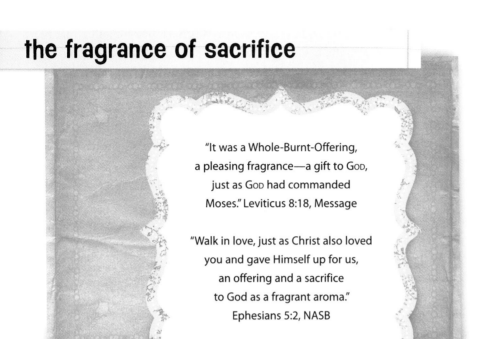

"It was a Whole-Burnt-Offering, a pleasing fragrance—a gift to GOD, just as GOD had commanded Moses." Leviticus 8:18, Message

"Walk in love, just as Christ also loved you and gave Himself up for us, an offering and a sacrifice to God as a fragrant aroma." Ephesians 5:2, NASB

As we viewed passages from Leviticus earlier in our study, we learned that God was specific about how sacrifices were to be offered. It was all about worship, legalities, and perfection in the offering. As we make our way through this how-to book for priests, it became apparent that true sacrifice is costly. Fourteen hundred years before Christ's birth, the Israelites offered time, money, and innocent blood along with the very best they had. God demanded this kind of sacrifice.

Fragrance, as revealed in Scripture, intrigues me. The Old Covenant was filled with instructions about releasing fragrance that was pleasing to God. Then Jesus became the final offering, making the system of the Old Covenant extinct. He became the offering, the pleasing fragrance that satisfied the heart of God.

Since Scripture repeatedly talks about aromas that are pleasing to God and refers to us as being "the fragrance of Christ" (2 Cor. 2:15; see additional references in "The Scripture Garden" on pages 134–35), how exactly can we release fragrance that is pleasing and sacrificial to Him? He has shown me one such way.

Years ago, my boys started shredding my heart as they began the natural process of leaving home. From college, to living on their own, to now—ripping up my emotions in ways I'd never imagined—walking off with my grandbabies! Any mama who has ever had to say good-bye to children totally gets this.

Early on, I frantically searched for ways to turn this hurt into something more noble than swollen eyes and a cavernous heart. During one of those searching moments, I walked by the bedrooms that only moments before had been cluttered with their belongings. Although the rooms lay vacant before me, my heart was anything but empty. The hole in my heart had been replaced with a suffocating boulder of melancholy. So it was truly a moment of divine rescue, as the Spirit spoke words of comfort to me. He made it strikingly clear to me that this heartache could be released to God Himself, through praise and thanksgiving. In fact, this was the only way I could deal with the pain of my children being gone, aside from falling headlong into the self-pity trap.

Incrementally, I've been learning that these moments are opportunities to release the fragrance of sacrifice to my Lord. Why sacrifice? Because it's a sacrifice to offer praise with a truly thankful heart when, at the moment, I only feel heartache. It's costly. I had to "give up my kids" to release this kind of fragrance.

God gets this. He gave up His dear Son for us. And Jesus, well, He gave Himself as a gift to God in becoming an offering for mankind. A pleasing sacrifice and a fragrant aroma diffused throughout heaven that day from Calvary. "Thanks be to God, who always leads us in triumph in Christ, and manifests through us the sweet aroma of the knowledge of Him in every place" (2 Cor. 2:14, NASB).

I'm experiencing to a greater degree that my joy is in Christ, not in my circumstances. Because of Him, it is possible to walk in victory when my life is crumbling. And when I do that, a sweet aroma lifts to my Heavenly Father. This knowledge gives purpose and holy opportunity to every life experience.

I invite you to seek the Father's guidance about making such an offering to Him. Whether it be past, present, or worries over future circumstances, you have opportunity right now to release a sweet fragrance to Him as you offer sacrifices dear to your heart. Bow your head and heart in worship, as you draw near to His altar.

Journal your experience as you feel led.

Dear Heavenly Father, I want to know more about how to offer my pain, trials, and heartache to You as a sacrificial offering. It's hard to rejoice when I don't feel like it. When I don't understand Your ways, it's so difficult to praise You, but I want to. I trust You, Lord. Show me how to sacrifice in praise so that I can release the fragrance of Christ to You and to a world in need. I love You.

resting on Sunday

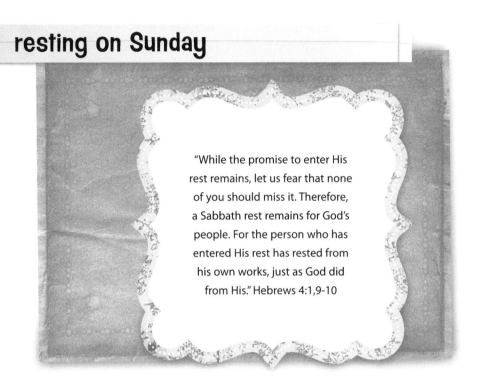

"While the promise to enter His rest remains, let us fear that none of you should miss it. Therefore, a Sabbath rest remains for God's people. For the person who has entered His rest has rested from his own works, just as God did from His." Hebrews 4:1,9-10

During my childhood years I rested much more on Sundays than I have in most of my adult life. Childhood made that possible but so did the Sunday lifestyle surrounding me. Stores, restaurants, movie theaters, and local businesses were closed. Not so true today. Twenty-first-century living, as a whole, neither values nor is conducive to resting. Because of our viral community, we are free to text, e-mail, shop, research, and simply play on the Internet seven days a week. Many of us don't even rest on vacations, filling every waking moment with activities to occupy our minds and bodies, leaving us more exhausted than before we left.

Still, the concept of resting on Sunday nags at believers who often wrestle with God's plan for resting on the Sabbath Day. So, what exactly does the Law God delivered to Moses have to do with us living in modern times?

The first mention of the Sabbath Day appears in Exodus 16:23. Moses explained to the children of Israel what the Sabbath was and how to keep it. They were to honor this day as a sign between them and God. In addition to resting this day, they were to reflect on their slavery in Egypt. This was a particular law set aside as a memorial between God and the people He'd brought out of bondage.

Jeremiah later prophesied that the law given at Mount Sinai would be replaced by a different law (see Jer. 31:31-32). The replacement of the law was Jesus Christ Himself. Since we live after the cross, we are not bound by the Sabbath and all the rules pertaining to it. Our commemoration of God's work in His Son, Jesus, comes not on the seventh day but the first day of the week, Sunday. Scripture tells us that Jesus' resurrection took place on a Sunday morning. "After the Sabbath, as the first day of the week was dawning, Mary Magdalene and the other Mary went to view the tomb" (Matt. 28:1).

As Christians, should resting be part of our celebration of Sunday? Personally, I believe it should for two reasons. First, God rested (see Gen. 2:2). Remember, He's God and certainly didn't need the rest. So for what other purpose did He rest than to lead us by example? And second, we need rest. No matter how energetic or on top of things you may be, you cannot keep going all the time. Physical, emotional, and just plain ol' dailyness will take you under without rest.

We live in the age of the Holy Spirit. He indwells us and counsels us of the things of God. "The Counselor, the Holy Spirit ... will teach you all things and remind you of everything I have told you" (John 14:26).

Here's the counsel I've been given, "Cindi, rest!" While writing this study, God has called me to pay attention to what I do on Sunday. He's called me to honor Him in a greater way than by simply going to church on the first day of the week. He's called me to turn this day into a day of reflecting and remembering what He did for me on the cross. Of course, I consider the cross every day, but on Sunday, I'm honoring Him by also resting my body and soul. I'm taking a break from the typical things that are a part of every other day of the week. Sometimes rest for me means doing family fun things and celebrating in activities with friends. And often He calls me to rest from the computer and phone. What's important is that I'm resting in Him and honoring Him as I do.

As we think about this rest concept, be very careful not to slip into legalism and come up with a set of rules as the Pharisees did. It helps me to think of do's instead of don'ts: *Lord, how can I relax and honor You on this day of celebration?*

There's simply no way to physically rest except by physically resting. There's no other way to relax your mind and emotions than to rest them. God knows that. I believe that's why He gave us the example. Resting our body and soul will also help us enter into His perfect rest, the place of peace, God's heart.

I challenge you to think about next Sunday. Talk to the Father about your plans to honor Him on this day. Record your thoughts.

Dear Father, I know Your Spirit is nudging me to rest. Please help me to honor You more than anything I have to do. Show me how to enter into rest and celebration in gratitude for all You have done for me. Help me to know that You will honor my commitment and enable me to get done the things I must get done on other days of the week. I am making a vow to You right now to set aside this day in thanksgiving, celebration, and rest.

If you have to work on Sundays, do things differently. Ask the Lord how you can set His day apart as holy as you work. He'll guide you in doing this and honor the gift of your heart in the midst of your work. If possible, devote another day of the week to resting as you would on Sunday if you didn't have to work.

Scribble your thoughts about resting on Sunday below.

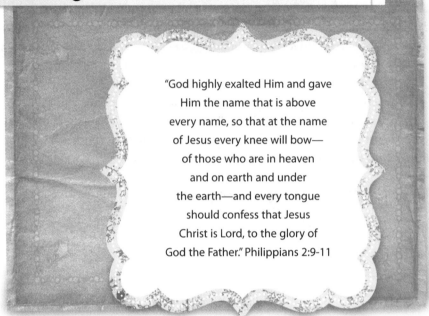

"God highly exalted Him and gave Him the name that is above every name, so that at the name of Jesus every knee will bow—of those who are in heaven and on earth and under the earth—and every tongue should confess that Jesus Christ is Lord, to the glory of God the Father." Philippians 2:9-11

Do you honor the name of Jesus? Do you speak His name with reverence, sincerity, and in a spirit of holy fear? It's likely that you do if you keep these verses from Philippians in mind. But way too often, the name of Jesus is thrown around casually without regard to the One behind the name.

Most of us were taught as children not to take God's name in vain. Exodus 20:7 in The Amplified Bible details what "in vain" means. "You shall not use or repeat the name of the Lord your God in vain, that is, lightly or frivolously, in false affirmations or profanely; for the Lord will not hold him guiltless who takes His name in vain."

This verse reaches far beyond using God's name attached to a curse word or mixed with profane verbiage. Misusing His name by using it lightly or frivolously is repeating His name in any context where you are not praying. For example, the phrase, "Oh Lord, I can't take any more of this" may be used as merely an expression by one who is fed up with it all. Or, the one speaking may be earnestly pouring out her heart to Jesus. It's all about your intention when you speak His name.

To use His name in prayer means that you are confident that He'd agree with what you are praying. It's saying, "My authority is in Jesus Christ, not anything or anyone else." Each time we pray His name, we send a message directly to the Devil that says, "I'm in the throne room, and I am praying with the authority of Jesus Christ by using His name!"

Remember, a legal transaction took place on the cross that day. Because that's true, Jesus said I could use His name to go before God for any need I have, including rebuking Satan. In this divine agreement I have with Him as His child, there is simply no room for disrespect.

Sadly, many Christians casually toss around God's name without giving any thought to Him at the moment, never realizing their grievous offense. God says, "You must not profane My holy name; I must be treated as holy" (Lev. 22:32).

The name of Jesus is no ordinary name—not because of the name but because of the One it represents. He is our Savior, our Lord, and our Holy God. Because of who He is, our proper posture before Him is one of holy trembling.

He's not "the man upstairs," "the big guy," or the "supreme commander." He's my dearest Friend but not in a pal-around kind of way. He's holy God. And my determination is to approach Him in holiness. First Peter 1:15-16 days, "As the One who called you is holy, you also are to be holy in all your conduct; for it is written, 'Be holy, because I am holy.' "

At the beginning of week 6, we talked about beholding God's glory by reading the visions of John as recorded in Revelation. As I daily spend time doing this, His holiness is becoming clearer and dearer to me. Fear of offending Him, however, is not what drives me. Instead, love compels me to approach my Lord and Savior with all the honor and glory due His name. I'm experiencing His tenderness, His grace, and His mercy in new waves of rhythm. Because of the depth of love He and I now share, my heart longs to please Him with every breath. And breathing His name with all the love and respect I can muster is the least I can do.

Join me in considering anew the name of Jesus. You can begin by thanking Him for the legal transaction that took place, making it possible for you to invoke His power by using His name. Praise Him that His name backs up all that He is. No greater love and power is available than to breathe the dear name of Jesus. "I am departing from the world; they are staying in this world, but I am coming to you. Holy Father, you have given me your name; now protect them by the power of your name so that they will be united just as we are" (John 17:11, NLT).

Record your thoughts.

Dear Father, in the name of Jesus, I bow before You. My heart adores You. I long to come in full submission to You, with every thought and every word I speak. Please reveal to me when I use Your name lightly or frivolously. That is not my desire. I repent of every time I've casually tossed Your holy name around. Please forgive me and accept my heart's gratitude for allowing me to breathe Your name in prayer. I love You.

silence and solitude

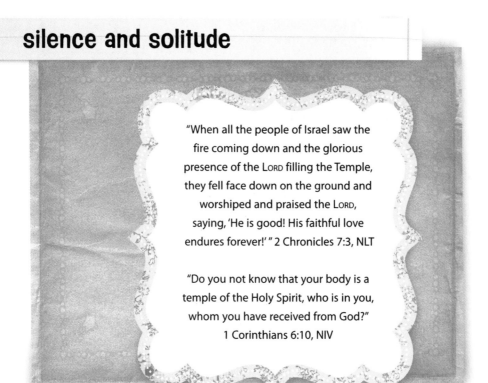

"When all the people of Israel saw the fire coming down and the glorious presence of the Lord filling the Temple, they fell face down on the ground and worshiped and praised the Lord, saying, 'He is good! His faithful love endures forever!' " 2 Chronicles 7:3, NLT

"Do you not know that your body is a temple of the Holy Spirit, who is in you, whom you have received from God?" 1 Corinthians 6:10, NIV

How important is it to practice silence and solitude?

It's critical! That is, if you're interested in restoring your sanity and staying the course in your journey to the cross.

Silence and solitude help you sink into the heart of God. Within His heart is where you square-off with the Enemy. Within His heart is where you learn to deal with the common daily stresses you face while living here on earth. As you learn to enjoy silence and solitude, you'll become less dependent upon spiritual goose bumps being the gauge of Christ's involvement in your life.

In my natural tendencies I have such an aversion to being alone and quiet. I enjoy engaging with people and seem to find much comfort in the whirring and buzzing of life going on around me. It's often awkward and uncomfortable and seems unnatural to pull away from it all.

Unnatural but biblical. Luke 5:16 states, "As often as possible Jesus withdrew to out-of-the-way places for prayer" (Message). Mark 6:31 also says "Because so many people were coming and going that they did not even have a chance to eat, he said to them, 'Come with me by yourselves to a quiet place and get some rest' " (NIV).

Jesus got it, and He still does. During His earthly life, He knew He must get away with His Father to keep refreshed and stay the course. He also knew how the demands of the crowds were pressing in on His followers and called them to get away in peace and quiet with Him. And, He knows all about you and the constant demands upon your life. So, He calls you to the place of refreshment and release.

I don't understand how, but I know it's a supernatural reality that stress and worry get swallowed up in worship. As I turn my focus from the turmoil in my mind to praise of my Heavenly Father, my mood lifts and my spirit is refreshed in the reality of Jesus.

Worship during silence and solitude is not getting away with Him to run down my list of prayer concerns. There's certainly reason to bring every concern to our Lord but only after worshiping Him. The more deeply I move into worshiping Him, the quicker I release my burdens.

When the Israelites saw the fire and smoke descend upon the temple, they were so awestruck that they simply fell down in worship. They weren't concerned with emptying their minds in prayer, as a lot of 21st-century teaching instructs. Rather, they were consumed with filling their minds with God's holiness.

For the believer in Christ, this is the reason for silence and solitude. He lives inside of you and is calling you to behold His glory. Your purpose is not to clear your mind and find yourself. Your one and only purpose is to worship holy God.

God loves you. You must not overlook this powerful truth. Therefore, you can trust Him to handle every life-consuming, energy-zapping event that comes your way. This trust is birthed and nurtured in silence and solitude through worship.

Your Counselor, the Holy Spirit, will rush to help you shut down (even for brief moments) to the chaos around you. Ask Him. He'll guide you in ways that fit your schedule and lifestyle. A favorite visual is that of Susannah Wesley, mother of famous brothers, John and Charles. Surrounded by 19 children in her small home, she often sat with an apron over her head. The children knew this was her time alone with God.[1] That's powerful imagery. I am learning to mentally toss my apron over my head when the clamor of life gets to me.

Sometimes you can get away from the crowds and noise; other times you can't. When that's the case, retreat to your temple on the inside. God lives there.

Use these suggestions as guidelines for your adventure in silence and solitude.

- **My personal favorite is early morning time with Him.** I am so enjoying this place of worship that I go to bed excited to get up. No tech stuff interrupts me and no day sounds distract me. I am free to engage in hearty worship, just Jesus and me.
- **Catch moments of solitude throughout your day.** You can always retreat emotionally and mentally with your Lord. It may be during your morning

shower that you welcome Him to refresh you as you offer Him the day ahead. It may be in the middle of clamor and chatter that you "shut-down" with Him for a few moments.

- **Try driving in silence.** Let the quiet soothe you as you listen for His voice.
- **Take a walk with a friend, in silence.** This is a great way to celebrate friendship and worship together.
- **Ask the Holy Spirit to counsel you** in using less words in your daily conversations. You'll be delighted at how doing this moves you into a place of peace.
- **Get away for an afternoon or a day.** Drawing away with Jesus from your normal environment will refresh you.

Right now, I'm praying for you to understand the holy value of entering into this spiritual discipline. It's not as difficult as you may think. Talk to Him about it. He'll gently invite you to this place of worship. Remember Matthew 11:28, "Are you tired? Worn out? Burned out on religion? Come to me. Get away with me and you'll recover your life. I'll show you how to take a real rest" (Message).

What are you thinking? Share any other insights you have as you complete this study.

Dear Heavenly Father, You alone know how difficult it is for me to withdraw to that quiet place with You. It's not because I don't want to; it's simply because of all the cares and demands on my life. Help me to see it's for my good and Your glory that I learn to get away with You. Encourage me as I take this step of obedience. Let me not grow weary of the distractions, only see them as stepping stones closer to Your heart. Here I come, Lord, with my heart surrendered and my soul abandoned.
I love You.

1. *Mothers of Influence* (Colorado Springs, CO: Honor Books, 2005), 27. Available from the Internet: http://books.google.com

how to become a Christian

God wants us to love Him above anyone or anything else because loving Him puts everything else in life in perspective. In God we find the hope, peace, and joy that are possible only through a personal relationship with Him. Through His presence in our lives we can truly love others, because God is love.

John 3:16 says, "God loved the world in this way: He gave His One and Only Son, so that everyone who believes in Him will not perish but have eternal life." To live our earthly lives "to the full" (John 10:10, NIV), we must accept God's gift of love.

A relationship with God begins by admitting we are not perfect and continue to fall short of God's standards. Romans 3:23 says, "All have sinned and fall short of the glory of God." The price for these wrongdoings is separation from God. "The wages of sin is death, but the gift of God is eternal life in Christ Jesus our Lord" (Rom. 6:23).

God's love comes to us right in the middle of our sin. "God proves His own love for us in that while we were still sinners Christ died for us!" (Rom. 5:8). He doesn't ask us to clean up our lives first—in fact, without His help we are incapable of living by His standards.

Forgiveness begins when we admit our sin to God. When we do, He is faithful to forgive and restore our relationship with Him. "If we confess our sins, He is faithful and righteous to forgive us our sins and to cleanse us from all unrighteousness" (1 John 1:9).

Scripture confirms that this love gift and relationship with God are not just for a special few but for everyone. "Everyone who calls on the name of the Lord will be saved" (Rom. 10:13). If you would like to receive God's gift of salvation, pray the following prayer.

If you prayed this prayer for the first time, share your experience with your small-group leader, your pastor, or a trusted Christian friend. To grow in your new life in Christ, continue to cultivate this new relationship through Bible study, prayer, and fellowship with other Christians. Welcome to God's family!

Dear God,
I know that I am imperfect
and separated from You.
Please forgive me of my sin
and adopt me as Your child.
Thank You for this gift of life
through the sacrifice
of Your Son. I believe Jesus
died for my sins. I will
live my life for You.
Amen.

scripture
garden

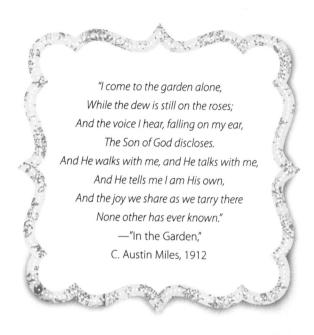

"I come to the garden alone,
While the dew is still on the roses;
And the voice I hear, falling on my ear,
The Son of God discloses.
And He walks with me, and He talks with me,
And He tells me I am His own,
And the joy we share as we tarry there
None other has ever known."
—*"In the Garden,"*
C. Austin Miles, 1912

Week 1: Psalm 42:1-2; 62:5-8; Matthew 6:33; 22:37; Mark 1:35; John 7:37; Romans 12:2; Revelation 21:6

Week 2: Proverbs 11:2; Isaiah 2:11; Zephaniah 2:3; 2 Corinthians 4:17-18; Galatians 6:14; Philippians 1:21; Colossians 3:2; James 4:6-8,10; 1 John 2:16

Week 3: Exodus 12:1-14; Leviticus 16:1-16; Jeremiah 29:13; John 1:14-18; 2 Timothy 2:19; Hebrews 5:13-14; 9:11-28; 1 John 1:1-10; Revelation 12:11

Week 4: 2 Samuel 7:28; Psalm 84:11; Proverbs 3:34; John 1:16-17; Romans 1:5, 11:6; 2 Corinthians 8:9; 12:9; Galatians 2:21; Ephesians 2:8

Week 5: Isaiah 61:1-3,10-11; Zephaniah 3:17; Matthew 7:25; John 10:9; 2 Corinthians 4:1-6; Ephesians 1:13-14; Hebrews 9:12; 1 John 2:25; Revelation 19:8

Week 6: Exodus 20:7; Psalm 16:9; 46:10; 62:1; 86:12; Habakkuk 2:20; Zephaniah 1:7; 2 Corinthians 2:14-15; Ephesians 5:2; 1 Timothy 1:17; Revelation 1:9-18; 4:1-11; 7:12

LEADER GUIDE

This leader guide will help you facilitate seven group sessions plus an optional seventh session for *Desperate: Seeking Simplicity … Finding the Cross*. Announce the study in the church newsletter, worship bulletin, on hallway bulletin boards, at women's ministry activities, and on your church's Web site and other social media outlets.

After you meet and get acquainted during session 1, be sure to complete each week's assignments before your next session. As the leader you do not have to have all the answers, but you need to be familiar with the material. Don't feel you have to cover every activity in this leader guide. Be flexible. Consider the personality of your group as you make decisions about which topics to discuss. Allow the Lord to lead your group discussions.

Join Cindi at *www.lifeway.com/women* for video clips, additional leader helps, and more. The study stands alone and can be done without these optional videos, but the videos may help you better facilitate *Desperate*. In these videos, Cindi briefly introduces the concepts that will be explored in each week's homework. Use these as desired or needed to add interest and depth to the study. Enjoy!

session 1

before the session
1. Watch Cindi's video to leaders at *www.lifeway.com/women* (optional).
2. Read "About the Author" (p. 4) and "Introduction" (p. 5). Be prepared to introduce the author, the study, and the format.
3. Have copies of *Desperate* ready for distribution.
4. Prepare a sheet for members' names, addresses, phone numbers, and e-mail addresses. Place it on a table with pens, markers, name tags, and a basket for collecting money for workbooks.
5. Decorate a bulletin board or poster to hold name tags between meetings.
6. Provide computer access to Cindi's videos if you choose to use them.

during the session
1. As participants arrive, ask them to sign in and pick up workbooks. If group members pay for their own workbooks, invite them to leave payment in the basket or offer to collect it after the session. Ask them to make a name tag. Collect these after each session as participants will be asked to decorate and use them in later sessions.
2. Welcome participants. Introduce yourself, giving participants a little information about you.
3. Briefly summarize the material about the author. Draw attention to the "Introduction" page, and explain unique features of the study such as the hymns, focus, and Scripture. Encourage participants to follow Cindi's direction to journal in "Scribble Your Thoughts" at the end of each day.

4. Show Cindi's introductory video to the study if you chose to participate in this option.

5. Ask participants why they chose to participate in *Desperate: Seeking Simplicity … Finding the Cross.* What would they like to have happen in their lives as a result? Ask: "What complicates your life? How do you try to simplify your life? How do you think the cross will change your focus?"

6. Remind everyone of meeting times. Emphasize the importance of individual study and group participation. Remind participants that all group discussions are confidential. Draw attention to "Totally Committed" (p. 144). Read the commitment together, and ask participants to sign the page as they commit to support each other during the study.

7. Watch the session 1 video of Cindi talking about what participants will study in week 1 available at *www.lifeway.com/women* (optional). Assign week 1 for the next small-group session. Explain that each week you will discuss the material participants have studied individually during the week. Encourage them to complete every learning activity to get the most out of their study and to continue participation in the group sessions even if they are not able to finish homework.

8. Close in prayer, asking God to give you an open heart as you commit to this study.

9. Ask participants to attach their name tags to the board you prepared before the session. Explain that you will use these name tags again as you explore what you have learned about seeking simplicity and finding the cross.

10. Encourage participants to worship throughout next week's study by singing "Jesus Loves Me."

session 2

before the session

1. Place the attendance sheet, name tags, pencils or pens, markers, and Bibles near the door. Have workbooks available for newcomers.

2. Complete the week 1 material.

3. Pray for participants by name.

4. Prepare to show Cindi's video if you choose this option.

5. Provide a player and music to "Jesus Loves Me," if desired.

during the session

1. As participants arrive, play "Jesus Loves Me" (optional). Ask them to sign in and get their name tags or prepare one.

2. Remind participants that the benefit of small-group study is to discuss the material studied together. Invite them to share questions and thoughts that occurred to them during the week.

3. Review the focus ("becoming desperate for God") and Scripture for day 1. "You're blessed when you're at the end of your rope. With less of you there is more of God and his rule" (Matt. 5:3, Message).

4. Review week 1 using the following discussion starters.

   a. Cindi mentions that a couple of stressors don't bother you, but they add up until someone or something sends you over the edge and you can't take any more. Ask participants to share how they handle that last straw. It may help others to know how to react—or not—in a future situation.

   b. Ask for volunteers to respond to Cindi's question, "Do we dare dream that it's possible to live a life free from the bondage of stress?" (p. 10).

   c. Discuss how one might move toward peace, joy, and fulfillment starting with the first critical step of having a desperation for your heart to mesh with the heart of God.

   d. Read the story of the blind beggar from Luke 18:35-43. Ask: "How did God speak to your heart in a fresh way?"

   e. Say: "Whether you slide into desperation gradually or are catapulted from the springboard of stress, this place can be a great place if it brings you to the end of self." Ask a volunteer to read Matthew 5:3 from The Message: "You're blessed when you're at the end of your rope. With less of you there is more of God and his rule."

   f. Ask members to share in groups of two or three a time they may have felt betrayed by God or may have had nowhere to turn except to Him. Suggest they read 2 Corinthians 4:9-10 together and commit to pray for each other this week.

   g. Discuss the biblical truth: "God has planted eternity in the human heart!" (see Eccl. 3:11). We have a craving that cannot and will not be satisfied with any earthly thing.

5. Watch the session 2 video of Cindi talking about what participants will study next week at *www.lifeway.com/women* (optional). Assign week 2 for the next group session.

6. Close by reading aloud Psalm 100, a psalm of thanksgiving.

7. Encourage participants to worship throughout next week's study by singing "At Calvary."

session 3

before the session

1. Complete the week 2 material.

2. Prepare the room for your group. Provide pencils, pens, and Bibles near the door.

3. If you like incorporating music into your small group, prepare to play "At Calvary" as women enter (optional).

4. Prepare slips of paper with these Bible verses: 2 Corinthians 5:12-21; 2 Corinthians 4:18; James 4:1; James 4:6; Colossians 3:2.

5. Post the definitions Cindi provides in week 2:

   center \ *verb* : focus on, revolve around, direct one's attention on something

   pride \ *noun* : a high or inordinate opinion of one's own dignity, importance, merit, or superiority

   vanity \ *noun* : excessive pride in one's appearance, qualities, achievements, and so forth

   rapture \ *noun* : ecstatic joy or delight; joyful ecstasy

   grace \ *noun* : the freely given, unmerited favor and love of God

   Consider leaving these posted and adding to them during the study.

during the session

1. Start music to "At Calvary" (optional) and welcome participants as they arrive and get their name tags. Ask them to draw a balloon that represents their stress level—0 is totally deflated and 10 is a huge pop!

2. Ask five willing readers to take a slip of paper with a Scripture reference.

3. Review the focus of day 1 ("returning to the cross").

4. Use the following discussion starters:

    a. Ask a volunteer to read 2 Corinthians 5:12-21. Ask: "What comforts and pleasures of home do you look forward to when you return home?" Ask for volunteers to share about times when God was drawing them into His presence.

    b. Ask a volunteer to read 2 Corinthians 4:18. Recall the words to "At Calvary" by saying or singing them together. Discuss the line in the hymn, "Caring not my Lord was crucified" and Cindi's conviction of never really having cared for what Jesus had done for her. Focus on her acceptance of God's immediate extension of grace.

    c. Ask a volunteer to read James 4:1. Repeat from the hymn, "Years I spent in vanity and pride." Discuss as a group where the line between appropriate guidelines ends and pride enters. Remind participants of Cindi's statement, "Our Savior never shouted 'What about Me?'" (p. 40).

    d. Ask a volunteer to read James 4:6. Read Cindi's statement, "It's important to consider self but within proper balance" (p. 42). Discuss what participants gleaned from day 4 regarding vanity and pride.

    e. Ask a volunteer to read Colossians 3:2. Discuss the definitions that Cindi provided in week 1.

    f. Invite participants to share how they actively share God's grace with others.

5. Watch the session 3 video of Cindi talking about what participants will study next week (optional) at *www.lifeway.com/women*. Assign week 3 homework for the next group session.

6. Close your time together in prayer. Ask the Lord to help you make each week's individual study and group participation a priority.

7. Encourage participants to worship throughout next week's study by singing "Nothing But The Blood."

session 4

before the session

1. Complete the week 3 material.

2. Pray for group members by name.

3. Prepare the room for your small-group session. Place pencils or pens and Bibles near the door.

4. Have a tear sheet or marker board and marker to compile members' responses to the word *blood*.

5. Post this definition Cindi provides in week 3.

guilt \ *noun* : remorse or self-reproach by feeling that one is responsible for a wrong or offense

6. If you like, prepare to play "There Is Power in the Blood" as women enter (optional).

during the session

1. Play "There Is Power in the Blood" (optional) as women enter.
2. Greet women as they retrieve their name tags (if needed).
3. Review the day 2 focus (moving in small steps of understanding) and Scripture (1 John 1).
4. Review week 3 using the following discussion starters:

   a. Compile members' words that came to mind when they heard the word *blood*.

   b. Discuss the statement, "Being in relationship with Jesus Christ means you are blood-bought and blood-covered" (p. 54).

   c. Have members discuss in pairs their thoughts and supporting Scriptures regarding God's pleasure at our cross quest. Ask them to share one thought with the group.

   d. Ask for volunteers to share their responses to "Remember This" (day 2, p. 58).

   e. Ask for responses to Cindi's definition of guilt: "Guilt (noun): remorse or self-reproach by feeling that one is responsible for a wrong or offense."

   f. Ask a volunteer to read Exodus 12:7. Point out the posted definition of *command*. Discuss the statements in "Action Was Required" (p. 66) concerning the Israelites' following God's instructions and the consequences they would have faced had they not obeyed.

   g. Ask for volunteers to share three advantages they've personally experienced because of living now instead of during Old Testament days. Post responses if desired.

5. Affirm members' participation. Watch the session 4 video of Cindi talking about next week's study at *www.lifeway.com/women* (optional). Assign week 4 for the next group session.
6. Close your time together in prayer.
7. Encourage participants to worship throughout next week's study by singing, "Grace Greater than Our Sin."

session 5

before the session

1. Complete the week 4 material.
2. Pray for each member and the group.
3. Prepare the room for your small-group session. Place pencils or pens and Bibles near the door.
4. Post the definitions Cindi provides in week 4.

legalism \ *noun* : strict adherence to law, especially to the letter rather than the Spirit

mercy \ *noun* : not getting what you deserve

grace \ *noun* : getting what you don't deserve

5. If you like, prepare to play "Grace Greater than Our Sin."

6. Write on a tear sheet the four statements from "The Spiritual Truth" (p. 94). Prepare this statement to post over them: "Every drop of Christ's shed blood is for you! There is no sin that is not covered by His sacrifice."

7. Consider printing and laminating Matthew 11:28-30 as a bookmark or memory card to give participants (optional).

during the session

1. Play "Grace Greater than Our Sin" (optional) as women enter.

2. Greet women by name as they arrive.

3. Review day 4 focus (applying grace to others) and Scripture (Matt. 11:28-30).

4. Review week 4 using the following discussion starters:

   a. Discuss thoughts women may have if they're trapped in a legalistic mind-set, noting new ones from participants (day 1, p. 77).

   b. Ask volunteers to share in general terms about a falling out with a good friend, restoration of relationship, and thoughts about the friendship (day 2, p. 80).

   c. Discuss two critical reasons to move into grace-living: (1) Grace cost Jesus His very life. By accepting what He so lovingly has given you, you honor Him. (2) When you understand what grace means to you personally, you are able and willing to offer it to others.

   d. Read Matthew 11:28-30: "Are you tired? Worn out? Burned out on religion? Come to me. Get away with me and you'll recover your life. I'll show you how to take a real rest. Walk with me and work with me—watch how I do it. Learn the unforced rhythms of grace. I won't lay anything heavy or ill-fitting on you. Keep company with me and you'll learn to live freely and lightly" (Matt. 11:28-30, Message). Ask members to prayerfully consider whether they need to get away with Jesus to recover their lives. Encourage them to remember this verse and go to God for rest in Him.

   e. Review the phrase "Freedom has everything to do with the 'unforced rhythms of grace'" (p. 89).

   f. Share what God is saying to you about the way you view others and what opportunities you have had to practice grace this week.

   g. Point out the definitions of mercy and grace and lead a discussion on members' response of when they either received or extended mercy and grace.

   h. Share as a group the three sentences members wrote about God and about themselves.

5. End with prayer, thanking God that "Every drop of Christ's shed blood is for you. There is no sin that is not covered by His sacrifice" (p. 94).

6. Watch the session 5 video of Cindi talking about what participants will study next week (optional) at *www.lifeway.com/women*. Assign week 5 for the next group session and ask participants to pay special attention to each day's focus.

7. Give women the bookmark or memory card with Matthew 11:28-30 on it as they leave (optional).

8. Encourage participants to worship throughout next week's study by singing "At The Cross."

session 6

before the session

1. Complete the week 5 material.

2. Pray for members and your group.

3. Prepare the room for your small-group session. Place pencils or pens and Bibles near the door.

4. If you'd like, prepare to play "At the Cross" (optional).

5. Post or prepare the five truth statements from day 2 (pp. 103–104) for volunteers to read.

during the session

1. Play "At the Cross" as women arrive (optional).

2. Greet women as they arrive.

3. Review week 5 using the following discussion starters.

    a. Ask participants which day's focus was most meaningful to them and why: (1) focusing on the cross; (2) understanding your security in Jesus; (3) enjoying your holy clothing; (4) understanding my responsibility; (5) understanding the nature of my relationship with Christ

    b. Discuss godly habits members have rooted in their lives, how they got them established, and how they would encourage a girlfriend to begin the same discipline (day 1, p. 99).

    c. Ask for volunteers to share a Scripture passage that has become more personal and meaningful to them during this study. Why is it significant?

    d. Review the truth statements from day 2.

    • Anyone who willingly and humbly repents of sin, embracing the truth of the cross and trusting Jesus as Lord and Savior, is saved.

    • If you have genuinely invited Jesus Christ into your heart as your personal Lord and Savior, you cannot lose your salvation.

    • Jesus' sacrifice was a one-time deal that covered every sin.

    • When we enter into salvation, God places His Holy Spirit within us.

    • Not accepting eternal security is refuting God's grace.

    e. Share how the awareness of wearing the robe of righteousness impacts members (day 3).

    f. Ask: "What steps will you take to match your lifestyle to your robe?" (day 4).

    g. Allow members to share a moment when they were exceptionally aware of God's glory and how they felt (day 5, p. 116).

4. Pray sentence prayers to end the session.

5. Watch the session 6 video of Cindi talking about what participants will study next week (optional) *www.lifeway.com/women*. Assign week 6 for the next group session.

Note from Cindi:

If time permits, I encourage you to allow a month before coming together again to wrap up study, asking participants to spend an entire month focusing on week 6 content. This will provide for individual needs being met according to the content. Ask them to mull over the idea of "The Scripture Garden," being prepared to share how they got involved with the Scriptures during the month. Lead them to be flexible and creatively sensitive to the Holy Spirit's leading.

session 7

before the session

1. Complete the week 6 material.
2. Prepare the room for your group session. Provide pencils or pens and Bibles.
3. If you like, prepare to play "Holy, Holy, Holy" (optional).
4. Because this week's material is different from others, follow especially closely the Holy Spirit in this session. Pray that you will hear His direction and be able to discern topics that best fit with your group.

during the session

1. Play "Holy, Holy, Holy" as participants enter (optional).
2. Ask participants to pick up their name tags. Say: "Here we are at the end of the study. We committed to look at our name tags at this stage and explore what we learned about seeking simplicity and finding the cross." Ask members how they would they draw their balloons differently now. How have their lives changed as a result of our study?
3. Invite members to share how they got involved with the Scriptures during the month. How were they able to be flexible and creatively sensitive to the Holy Spirit's leading?
4. Close in prayer.

totally committed

I, _____,
commit to my Father, my Bible study partners, and myself to:

1. **Love the Lord with all my heart, soul, and mind.**
2. **Seek first His kingdom throughout this study.**
3. **Complete the assignments before each group meeting.**
4. **Pray for the women in my group.**
5. **Keep the confidential matters discussed within the group session confidential.**
6. **Be open and obedient to the Holy Spirit's promptings.**

Signature/Date: _____

Signatures of group members:

_____   _____

_____   _____

_____   _____

_____   _____

_____   _____

_____   _____

_____   _____